ALL Business is STILL
Show Business

● ● ●

ALL Business is STILL Show Business

Create Distinction and Earn Standing Ovations From Customers in a Hyper-competitive Marketplace

15th Anniversary Edition

Scott McKain

ISBN-13: 9781542858038
ISBN-10: 1542858038
Library of Congress Control Number: 2017901510
CreateSpace Independent Publishing Platform
North Charleston, South Carolina

Table of Contents

Foreword

The original reason I wrote this book is because I was leading a double life.

OK, I realize that sounds more intriguing than the reality of the situation. I wasn't a spy, or hiding some kind of dark secret, or anything that would make for an exciting plot in an international movie thriller. Instead, I simultaneously had two occupations that seemed, at first glance, to be totally diverse from one another.

Back in the 1980's, I was beginning my career as a professional speaker. I spent a significant amount of my time preparing the content for the programs and presentations I was delivering. I also expended a great deal of effort marketing and selling my services to launch my fledgling small business. As a young entrepreneur, I was constantly searching for new ideas and concepts that would provide me a strategic advantage in the marketplace to help me close a higher percentage of proposals, and serve my clients more effectively. This effort was not only undertaken for my long-term success. I needed to keep food on the table and a roof over the head of my new spouse and me as we started our marriage!

Because of a fortuitous circumstance, a network syndicator offered me the opportunity to appear every week on over eighty television stations in the United States, Canada, and Australia as a movie reviewer. Not only would thousands of people around the world watch me each week as I gave my thoughts on the latest films – it meant I would have the chance to privately and personally interview the greatest stars in show business: Tom Hanks, Meryl Streep, John Travolta, Bruce Willis, Arnold Schwarzenegger, and many more.

As I moved back and forth, from one life to another, from corporate presentations to show business reviews, I found myself discovering that:

* There was more in common between the "typical/traditional" business and the entertainment industry than many on either side recognized.
* Areas where the entertainment industry was enjoying tremendous success were precisely the points where many organizations in other industries were struggling.
* The global culture – not just in the United States where I reside – was experiencing the enormous impact of the entertainment industry.
* And, that this phenomenon was occurring to such a degree, it was altering the expectations of our customers in ways that were only beginning to be understood.

In response to these new ideas (and more) that I was having, I started trying to find a way to bridge these two worlds that I was dividing my time between. The result was that I started asking the celebrities questions about the elements of their success, discipline, artistry, and achievement. Simultaneously, I began examining how individual professionals and visionary organizations might employ some of the strategies and practices of show business to create more compelling experiences for their customers, in order to enhance client loyalty and company profitability.

Initially, I was attempting to create an edge in the marketplace for *my* small business. Eventually, I realized that what I was learning through my research and examination was creating an approach to, and philosophy about, business that could benefit – *sometimes to an extraordinary degree* – every professional and any organization in all industries.

I refined the idea, then started presenting speeches and seminars on my concept – which I titled, "ALL Business is Show Business." Well before the release of terrific books that examined this phenomenon like, *The Experience Economy* and others, I was speaking to groups around the United States about my philosophy.

About fifteen years later – inspired, in part, by the publishing legend Mel Berger of William Morris Endeavor -- and mentored by Larry Stone, formerly of Rutledge Hill Press – I finally wrote the original edition of the book.

The reception to the initial version was interesting, to say the least. Even though I took great pains to show that this book was not about "glitz and glamour," there were some readers who responded with comments such as, "I'm not in show business. I make and sell widgets." (If that's what *you* are thinking, don't worry. One of my goals for this book is to help you perceive your business a bit differently.)

Much has changed in the over thirty years since my original concept and speech – and the fifteen-plus years since the initial writing and publication – of the book, *ALL Business is Show Business*. Both my research and my practical experience tell me that this topic has *never been more important* to the individual success of extraordinary professionals. And, it has never been more critical regarding the growth and achievement of every organization -- regardless of the size of your business or marketplace in which you work.

For the last several years, my work has centered on creating distinction. I've been researching and learning how organizations and individual professionals can stand out and move up in these hyper-competitive times. I'm fascinated with what it takes to be distinctive in any marketplace.

That's why this new version of *ALL Business is Show Business* is not a "re-write" or "updated edition." Think of it more like the James Bond franchise when the actor playing the superspy changed from Pierce Brosnan to Daniel Craig. The producers didn't just keep making the same type of

Bond movie with a different performer. Instead, they did a total "re-boot" of the series.

The result was that the familiar character of James Bond took on an entirely different perspective. Audiences responded by making the longest running series of sequels in the history of motion pictures more popular (and profitable) now than ever.

In other words, this isn't "ALL Biz is Show Biz Redux." Instead, it's "ALL Biz is Show Biz Reboot!" This new (or, perhaps, "new-*ish*") book will seriously consider the extraordinary challenges that are facing all of us in business on how to differentiate ourselves from the competition. And, because it's obvious that these concepts are more important than ever, I've altered the title a bit to remind us that "all business is *STILL* show business!"

When a reality-show television host is elected President of the United States — regardless of whether you support or oppose his political positions — it displays the depth in which we are experiencing this phenomenon that I've been discussing for years.

The obstacles to our success and growth in this new marketplace of instant gratification, immediate access to information, and global online competition naturally generates this vital question:

The most important question that any business or any professional can be asking today is this*: "How can my customers tell the difference between us and the competition?"*

If customers can't tell a difference between you and other viable alternatives — why *shouldn't* they choose another option?

However, if your approach is more appealing, more compelling, and engages more significantly with them— just as a hit movie or television show will accomplish for their specific audience — then, you will become their distinctive preference.

As you advance through this book, you'll learn specific strategies and precise tactics that may be of immense value in assisting you to distinguish yourself in the marketplace.

In other words, those who are most adept at executing the "ALL Business is STILL Show Business approach" will naturally find themselves creating distinction in their respective marketplace.

Thank you for investing your time and making the effort to learn the steps to create distinction and deliver the Ultimate Customer Experience through the principles of *ALL Business is STILL Show Business!* My strong desire is that you will find the concepts and strategies outlined here to be of significant value.

Scott McKain
Las Vegas, Nevada
February 1, 2017

Introduction: What Makes a "Show Business" Succeed?

Does it seem as though your customers are less loyal and more demanding? Do the people who buy your products and services now want it better, quicker, and cheaper – no matter how tough it is for you and your organization to deliver?

Have your employees changed? Perhaps you feel the work ethic of your colleagues is different than it used to be.

How about you – and your professional standing? Could you benefit from a greater ability to "connect" with your customers and colleagues? Does your communication to them sometimes seem ignored or lost in the clutter?

If any - or all - of these examples sound familiar, you are experiencing the impact of the cultural phenomenon this book will tackle.

* **In today's culture, we are relentlessly bombarded with entertainment.**
* It has reached the point that we have created a culture of customers who now expect a compelling experience whenever and wherever they do business.

* Perhaps we could even make the case that the most recent Presidential election displayed that the "experience" created by the candidate who was victorious transcended his or her ability to espouse specific facts or information about policy.

The purpose of this book is to show you how to leverage the secrets that the entertainment industry employs to create persuasive emotional connections with their audiences, so that you can generate that same manner of distinctive, loyal engagement with your customers.

Whether it is the latest television hit like *Empire* or a classic movie that we stream from Netflix – from Howard Stern on satellite radio that millions listen to daily, to a hit podcast like *Serial* where millions of listeners download each installment – Jimmy Fallon or Jimmy Kimmel – CNBC to ESPN – the entertainment industry surrounds us.

My belief after decades of speeches and seminars to the leading corporations of the world -- and after a decade as an entertainment reviewer interviewing the icons of Hollywood -- is that show business has inundated us so thoroughly, it has changed the very nature of how we buy and work.

If you do not understand this principle – and change the way you relate to customers and employees accordingly – you are going to fail, individually and organizationally.

Here's one of the most important points to understand about show business:

* **Entertainment succeeds when it establishes an emotional connection with the audience. The more powerful the connection, the greater the success.**

Entertainment does *not* mean merely laughter and song.

As one friend asked, "Is my cardiologist in show business? I mean, I don't want him to tap dance his way to my by-pass!" If that is what you are thinking – perhaps you have a narrow view of the entertainment industry!

Certainly, at times and in appropriate situations, the response desired is amusement. However, you would not even begin to think that the purposes of a product of the entertainment business like the classic old movies, *Schindler's List* or *Silence of the Lambs* – or more recent hits like *American Sniper* or *12 Years A Slave* -- was to create a sense of light-hearted fun and slapstick mirth.

The same is true in *your* business. For some organizations, creating and enhancing a connection with your customers and employees -- your audience, if you will -- *will* be found through increased humor and fun. Others -- like an accounting firm or B2B-type organization -- will establish their emotional bond through caring, concern, and identification with the client's specific challenges, as well as their customers and employees.

*   **A critical point to remember is that you must establish a passionate linkage with your clients and colleagues to create the type of loyal relationship that *every* business is seeking with its most important targets.**

It has never been more prevalent or powerful. As you read this book, keep the recent Presidential election in the back of your mind. I'd strongly suggest that Donald Trump understood these principles – and executed upon them – significantly more aggressively than Hillary Clinton. It's part of why he won an election that many pundits and professionals presumed he would lose.

For example, there's no arguing that Donald Trump is nothing else if not a "showman." Some pundits attributed a decline in the television ratings for broadcasts of the NFL in the 2016 season to viewers tuning out football games so they could tune in a Trump speech or interview. His flair for publicity and grabbing attention not only helped him attain the White House, but fame and fortune as a real estate developer earlier in his life and career, as well.

It's important to note – this is *not*, in any manner whatsoever, meant to condone or condemn any of Mr. Trump's policies or pronouncements.

This is not a book about politics. It is critical, however, to observe that an election is much like a business. Every political campaign is about compelling prospects (called "citizens") to go to the polls and make a commitment. This process is not unlike your business, where you try to persuade prospects to make a commitment (called a "purchase") from you, instead of your competition.

* If you abhor the policies of Donald Trump, you should even be more motivated to understand the principles he used to achieve victory so your side can win the next election.
* If you support his approach and the direction he wants to take the United States, it should compel you to learn the cultural shifts and changes that made his triumph possible.

(To enhance the point about the relevance of "show business" -- as of this writing, Mr. Trump's nominee to be the Secretary of Treasury and at the point position running the nation's economy is Steven Mnuchin. Mr. Mnuchin's qualifications for the position include 17 years at Goldman Sachs and as chief executive of Dune Capital Management, a privately-owned hedge fund. However, show business is part of his background, as well. He financed the recent movie, *Suicide Squad* – and was executive producer of many films such as *American Sniper, Sully,* and *Mad Max: Fury Road.* Understanding and implementing the concepts from this book is germane on Sunset Boulevard, Wall Street...and the Main Street of every city and town.)

There are movies that I love...that friends of mine despise: not everyone likes the same thing. (I was aghast to recently learn that a pal of mine is totally indifferent about the *Star Wars* movies. To each his own, I guess.)

Yet, just because something is not your "cup of tea" does not mean that you cannot -- or should not -- *learn from its success.* You don't have to love the character of Walter White or the television program *Breaking Bad* to leverage it into a lesson about how to tell a story, or how to evolve a character.

The book you have in front of you will examine this phenomenon and explain how you can make it work for you and your organization. We will also discuss why it is so significant. In addition, you'll find specific steps prescribed that you and your business can take to sell and serve your customers -- and manage and motivate your employees -- more productively in this world of hyper-connectivity and hyper-competition.

It's SHOWTIME!

Chapter 1

* * *

Setting the Stage: Your Business IS Show Business

They say you should never stop learning...

S everal years ago, I experienced an incident that changed my beliefs about the way that you and I should do business. That event -- together with the extensive research I have conducted into hundreds of organizations -- inspired me to develop my business philosophy:

* **ALL business is, in effect, "show business."**

* No matter what your organization does
* No matter what your distribution channels are
* No matter what services you offer or what products you manufacture
* No matter whether you are a CEO or a new sales representative
  o YOUR business has become "show business."

Yes...your business *is* show business.

Remember the singer John "Cougar" Mellencamp? He is now a member of the Rock and Roll Hall of Fame and continues to tour and play to sold out theatres around the world. Perhaps you recall some of his hit songs, like "Jack and Diane," "Pink Houses," "R.O.C.K. in the USA" – or, maybe even my favorite -- "Small Town"?

When this rock star begins to sing that last song with the opening line, "I was born in a small town," I have a heightened sense of pride. You see, I was born in the *same* small town. In fact, John recorded part of the video for the song near my home farm.

John went to school in the city of our birth, Seymour, Indiana. I – a few years later -- attended the even smaller Crothersville High School.

I start this book with my distant linkage to a rock and roll icon for a simple reason. If you recall any of Mellencamp's old music videos -- or want to check them out on YouTube -- it might assist you to envision the small community where I spent my youth. It is the home of around 1,400 people about 35 miles north of Louisville, Kentucky. My hometown may not sound like the most likely birthplace of a business philosophy – especially one about the impact of "show business!" However, an event that took place there changed the way I would look at organizations forever.

I donated a day to return to Crothersville to give a presentation. The event was a meeting to help motivate and uplift the school's teachers and administrators that was held the day before the students arrived to begin a new school year.

I must admit that well before the program even started I was already feeling scared to death. Sitting in the front row was one of my former teachers!

Part of the problem I experienced came from my memories of the tremendous crush that I had during my elementary school years on this then-cute, petite 22-year-old teacher!

On my trip back home, I naturally looked forward to seeing her again. The image of her in my mind was naturally the way she looked when I was in school.

Imagine my shock to see her now -- 65 years old -- and noticing that her stretch pants had no choice! Of course, she was just as shocked...standing in front of her was not the skinny, bespectacled eight-year-old kid with the "flat-top" haircut of her memories. It was a middle-aged guy with a beard, longer hair, and not in such great physical shape, either!

We both laughed about how the years had affected our respective appearances – then, it was time for the meeting to begin.

I was more than just a little nervous to speak in front of the educators who had meant so much in my life. So, I decided to start my presentation with a standard question that many speakers and authors will ask to begin a lecture: "Let's start by having you tell me," I said, "what is the single biggest problem in education today?"

It is easy to anticipate how the program participants are going to respond. And, on this occasion, I convinced myself that I knew the answers that these teachers were going to provide.

I expected that the teachers in the audience were going to cite these four as their biggest problems:

1. *the discipline of the students*
2. *encouraging the involvement of parents*
3. *drug, alcohol, and violence problems in American schools*
4. *governmental funding challenges in education*

Imagine my surprise when my former teacher raised her hand and declared, "Scott -- I believe the biggest problem in education today is *'Sesame Street!'*"

I immediately responded with a profound, *"Huh?"*

Calmly, my former educator asked me, "Scott, who taught you the alphabet?"

I answered truthfully, "Well, my mother and my grandmother."

"Of course," she said. "I remember. However, for the last three decades and more, young people have been taught their alphabet by characters like Big Bird, and Bert & Ernie."

"That means," she continued, "that they arrive on the steps of this school for their first day of formal instruction *expecting to be entertained as they are educated.*"

"Wow!" I thought. Then I realized, my elementary school teacher was *still* teaching me.

* *For the past three decades and more, we have taught almost everyone in this culture that education -- as well as training, selling, motivating, managing, serving and everything else that a business is supposed to do, and everything else that is supposed to happen in life -- is going to be entertaining.*
* *We have – intentionally or not – ingrained in almost <u>every</u> person the expectation that everything we do should be wrapped in an experience.*

Here's an important point to state at beginning: the scope of how we were taught through narrative is universal. That means that the "ALL Business is Show Business" philosophy works for you whether you are a sales professional or manager – an executive with a "blue chip" corporation or an entrepreneur with a tiny, one-person business – flashy and outgoing, or serious and studious. This philosophy works for organizations *and* individuals.

This concept is worth spending your time and effort to consider. Because we have been so engaged and enthralled with narrative on such an intensive basis for such an extended period in both our leisure and our labor, the importance of creating this type of connection with both customers and employees has only enhanced in importance over the years. According to Facebook, video uploads from the United States to their site increased by 94% from 2014 to 2015. Video views went from 4 billion per day to 8 billion per day during 2015! The data clearly demonstrates we are craving video, stories, and narrative.

And, when you consider the dramatic impact of the Millennial generation in the marketplace, you will discover that the "ALL Business is Show Business" philosophy isn't just a technique to create a distinctive approach. It may become the only way to survive in a hyper-competitive marketplace!

Rebooting YOUR business to show business

I mentioned earlier that this was a "reboot" of my work on *ALL Business is Show Business*. May I suggest the same needs to be true of your efforts? Unless you reboot, reorganize, and recast your efforts to attract this changing customer, your organization is nothing short of doomed!

In an issue of his "Trend Letter," noted *Megatrends* author John Nesbitt wrote several years ago, "Want to sell, train, manage, motivate? First, you must *entertain*. In today's world of change, entertainment is now assumed to be an integral factor in everyday life."

The United States Chamber of Commerce, in their magazine *Nation's Business*, featured a cover story entitled "Entertailing." This word is a combination of "entertainment" and "retailing." The essence of the article is that if you are not adding the factor of entertainment to your business, *your organizational goose is beginning to cook.*

I have been traveling the world emphasizing this point in speeches and seminars for three decades. That is why it was especially gratifying to see an article in the *Harvard Business Review* that agreed with what I have been saying all along: The corporation is primarily a stage upon which you "showcase" for your customers, employees, and prospects.

Distinctive, visionary organizations understand this principle. Simply stated, they "get it."

Ask yourself, "What is Nike's business?"

If you were from the old style of business thinking, you probably would say that Nike's business is the "shoe business." With apologies to someone perhaps only remembered by the older American readers of this book -- the late, great television variety show host, Ed Sullivan -- it is not "shoe business." It is *show* business!

Nike's business is a lifestyle business. Nike understands their business is not merely about shoes, or other varied athletic apparel, as might be easily misunderstood. It is lifestyle.

We should note that when Nike's competitors – such as Adidas – moved their brands from being about performance shoes into fashion experiences for the physically fit (and those who want to be), they started making inroads into Nike's dominance in the marketplace.

The NPD Group reported that in 2016, sales for "classics" and "casual athletic" shoes were up – while "basketball" shoe sales plummeted. The move away from the traditional approach of focusing on specific types of shoes -- and into creating an experience around lifestyle -- paid dividends for those who adopted this approach. I would suggest the same is true of other distinctive organizations in varied industries -- like Starbucks, Disney, and Zappos.

Creating emotional connections with YOUR audience

ALL Business is STILL Show Business is NOT going to be about spending more money and blowing out your budget. It is not just about "fun," and it is certainly not superficial. Instead, this approach for your products and services – just like the entertainment industry successfully employs for hit movies, television programs and more -- is about establishing and communicating through an emotional connection with a designated audience.

It is not about dressing up in funny costumes and playing silly games. It is not even about "entertaining your customer" in the way that many organizations do – taking them to dinner or sporting events.

It IS about how you connect with the people who are most important to your business – your customers and colleagues. It is about understanding the need for high-touch solutions in a high-tech world.

> * **It's about realizing that emotional engagement and relationships are more profitable than a mere sale.**

In today's world, these customers are taking product quality and service commitment for granted. Now, they are increasing their demands and raising the benchmark again. They are now saying, "Great is NOT good enough! If you want my business, amaze me! Knock me out!"

("Great," in fact, is not nearly "good enough." In a previous book of mine, *Create Distinction: What to Do When 'Great' Isn't Good Enough to Grow Your Business*, it is shown that ten of the eleven companies that were cited as the "great businesses" in the bestselling business classic, *Good to Great* are no longer market leaders – even to the point of bankruptcy, liquidation, and securities fraud.)

In other words, these customers -- raised in a culture where they expected to be entertained as they were being educated -- now expect to be entertained as they are sold, served, informed, trained, and employed. The emotional bonding that we discussed earlier is the single most important element that you can build in to your professional relationships in today's marketplace.

• • •

Show Biz Quiz

* On a sheet of paper, answer the following question: If you were being chosen to go on a trip to Mars and was confined to a spacecraft for six months, what four movies would you take along?
  o Remember, these are not necessarily the four films that you believe are the greatest movies ever made. These are the four feature films you could watch over and over again for six months.
* Save your answers – we will examine them further in a moment.

• • •

This is not a superficial issue

It is critical that we emphasize at the outset that when we are discussing "show business," we are not discussing a frivolous endeavor. The old cliché in Hollywood is that they do not call it "show *art*." They call it "show *business!*"

In my home country of the United States, agriculture was formerly the nation's primary hope for balancing the national trade deficit. Now, the entertainment industry provides a significant percentage of our exports. Hollywood tracks how well a movie opens in Bangalore with as much intensity as the box office receipts from Baltimore.

This is not to suggest that we should rush to dismiss the "fun factor," however. If "ALL Business is Show Business" sounds like heresy, consider the following shocking statistic. I recall being on a panel several years ago, when another speaker announced that the Retail Marketing Institute released a study revealing, in essence, that *over 70% of customers said they would tend to go someplace else to make a purchase if it was "more entertaining" to do business elsewhere.*

Even if my memory isn't perfect regarding the precise percentage, I will never forget being amazed by the general point of the statistic. More "entertaining"? *More "fun"?* What about those products we have worked so hard to engineer? What about those employees we have spent millions to train? What about all the things I learned in business school or management training that were supposed to make a difference to the customer?

To rephrase an earlier point, this philosophy does not mean that you need to become a stand-up comedian as a CEO or manager. Your customers and employees are not looking for a "floor show." Inserting the entertainment factor into your products and services -- and making your business a "show business" -- is not about balloons and costumed characters. It is not mere frivolity.

While the products of show business might stereotypically be associated with enjoyment, it is vitally important to remember that "fun" is not the same as "frivolous." As stated earlier, show business is a very serious enterprise. One of the important points we learn from show business is that we should take our products and our organizations very seriously.

The difference is that the successful show business enterprise does not take *itself* too solemnly. The suggestion here is that while we should be serious about our products and services, more organizations need to understand they should not be so grim about themselves or their image.

> * **It is a business _philosophy!_ And, it works for entrepreneurs and small business just as powerfully as it does for major corporations.**

This book will present these steps somewhat informally so you may customize them to your specific and unique situation. However, you can think of the "ALL Business is Show Business" philosophy as a five-step approach to making your business – and you – more compelling in the marketplace:

1. Begin to perceive YOUR business as "show business" – and that your goal is to create distinction through compelling emotional connections with customers and colleagues
2. Develop a High Concept for your company, department, specific projects – and yourself – to enhance the precision of your focus and become exceedingly clear about your uniqueness in the marketplace, who you are, and what you can deliver.
3. Craft a persuasive story (or stories) to deepen and enrich emotional connectivity with a more powerful and memorable approach.
4. Pay special attention to the pacing of the customer's interaction with you – and how that can focus their attention in a manner that will obtain mutually successful outcomes.
5. Prepare yourself – and educate your team – in the techniques of performers creating emotionally engaging experiences, not just as employees executing the functions of their jobs.

Yes, _your_ business is show business.

Chapter 2

● ● ●

Why Show Business Should Be the Model for YOUR Business

*T*he benchmark is rising in business. It tells us that a major new revolution is happening right now among customers and employees.

Compare our current situation to what happened in the automobile industry in the United States in the 1970's. Back in the '70's, Japanese car manufacturers came to America and revolutionized the car business. Just about every study conducted at that time suggested that customers considered the Japanese product to be of a higher quality than its American counterpart.

What happened next? Detroit went to work and re-engineered their cars to meet the new, and higher, customer demands. They did such a great job, that many customers now assume that the American and Japanese cars are approximately equal in terms of product quality. In fact, younger generations like Millennials and Gen X probably don't remember a time when the quality of many American cars was so suspect.

At that point -- where the quality of American cars was dramatically improved after many years of inferior workmanship -- did customers then collectively exclaim, "That's great! Just about every manufacturer now has a high-quality product, so I won't ask you for anything else!"

Of course not. Not at all! Customers instead *raised their level of expectations once again.*

Is this result what automotive manufacturers *wanted* to occur? It doesn't matter – their feelings here are irrelevant. Their customers raised the benchmark for them. What transpired at this point in history was that customers proclaimed, "I have a higher quality product. Now...I want better *service!*"

"Customer service" then became the name of the game in the automotive industry. This is when we started to see car dealers stay open later. (Some service bays even began to remain open until midnight!) Customers could feel a concerted effort in terms of enhancing the level of service provided by the manufacturer and the dealership.

It was fascinating to note several years ago when General Motors added "roadside assistance" to segments of their product line. If you run out of gas, you get on your mobile phone, call GM and they will bring gas to you. If you have a flat tire -- even in your own driveway -- they will come fix it! As a sign of continued leadership, the first automobile brand to provide in-car, 4G Wi-Fi connectivity in the United States was not Mercedes or Lexus -- it was Chevrolet!

Consider for a moment that it was not too many years earlier that the only automotive manufacturers with a roadside assistance plan were Mercedes, Lexus, and Rolls Royce. Now you can get it on your GM car. This was clearly a revolution in the automotive business.

Here is an important question: Is it being reasonable to expect your customers to stop raising their demands?

The answer is an emphatic, "**No.**"

(You might *wish* they would stop elevating their requests...but, we both know they will not. Are you willing to lower your expectations when YOU are the customer?)

Customers are now saying that they assume that you have a quality product – otherwise, you would be out of business in these changing and competitive times. In addition, they are saying if you do not have a modicum of service, you probably have already gone to the wayside as well.

What is your definition of service?

"Over seventy percent of companies believe customer service has improved over the past five years," said an article in an old issue of Delta Airlines *Sky* magazine that I recall. An equally high percentage of customers believe that service has *declined*. How can this be true?

The corporate world frequently holds the conviction that "efficiency" is synonymous with "service." An executive with one of my clients was bragging to me before a recent presentation that they had improved their "service" levels. To prove his point, he stated they were now answering the phone before the third ring, and delivered product orders within forty-eight hours. What he could not understand was why customers were not becoming more loyal.

* **The problem was that customers were using a different measuring stick.**

Oftentimes, we blend the word "service" with the term "experience." In fact, those are two different points on a continuum.

For example, let's imagine that you go to the theatre and discover that it is well maintained and clean. The popcorn is fresh and promptly served. This means that you have had good *service*. However, if the movie is terrible and you feel as though you wasted your time and money, you haven't had a good *experience* – regardless of the snacks at the concession stand.

In other words, the vast differences in accurate definitions are creating the vastly different perceptions about service. And, as we will explore later in this book, customers do not become "raving fans" (to use the term of author Ken Blanchard) over "service." It requires an extraordinary "experience" to generate the customer loyalty that every organization – and customer -- desires.

• • •

Show Biz Quiz

Take another look at your four movies for the trip to Mars. What emotions do they arouse in you?

For example, the four films I would take are:

* *Tombstone* – a movie that has it all; love of family and friendship, winning in spite of enormous odds, and trying to recover a love that seemed lost.
* *Young Frankenstein* – just flat-out funny – and would keep my spirits up.
* *Schindler's List* – one man's passion can change the lives of countless others.
* *Taken* – hey, a guy must take one action movie! And, this is one of the all-time great action pictures.

I am certain your list is different; yet, I would bet there are similarities. Just four films can raise an almost infinite amount of emotions. From tears to laughter, from nail-biting excitement to desperation, your choices and mine prove that show business can create powerful emotional connections.

Look at your four films, and describe on your sheet of paper the emotions that your choices arouse in you.

• • •

Just another instance...

Let's examine one illustration of how the "show business" philosophy applies to what ALL of business is trying to do. "Outsourcing" has become a major topic because of the intense efforts to manage costs. Jobs that were previously performed by full-time employees are now being performed by outside vendors. This is absolutely nothing new to the movie business. If you examine how a movie is made, you will find that a film production is actually a multi-million-dollar corporation.

You may recall the drama surrounding the classic hit film *Titanic* that started well before the movie's release. Many insiders in show business staged heated debates about the financial wisdom of making the movie. Even the man who directed, produced, and wrote the movie joked about the decision.

Jim Cameron asked me during an interview to imagine his pitch to the studios for financing. As he put it, here was a movie where, "There is no chance for a sequel, the audience knows the ending, and most of the characters die in the end."

The two movie studios underwriting the production undertook an enormous risk, as the film's budget went well over $200 million (a figure that would be $300 million in US dollars in 2017). At the time of its release in 1997, it was the most expensive movie ever made. It also became, at the time of its release, the biggest box office hit of all time.

Consider for a moment how the money was spent. The actors and technical professionals – ranging from camera operators to sound editors – are all independent contractors. Most those who built the sets, created the enhanced graphics on computers, and played the instruments in the orchestra recording the soundtrack were professionals who were not employees of the studios that produced *Titanic*.

The film was, in essence, a billion-dollar company that was staffed almost exclusively by outsourced professionals.

I am not suggesting here that all business is going evolve into all of us being freelancers. However, several years ago an important article from *Fast Company* introduced us to the concept that many of us are becoming "free agents." (Not to mention that it introduced many of us to future best-selling author Daniel Pink!) In other words, these articles are suggesting that we all work for ourselves.

All any company does for an employee is to "rent" that person's time, talent, services, and abilities. In the past, these "employee services" were traditionally "rented" by the employee to only one company. The "free agent" concept hypothesizes that we are moving into renting our services to multiple employers for varying lengths of time.

The movie business has been applying this structure for many years. It is a great example of how a business of the future will be managed, funded, and administered.

● ● ●

Show Biz Quiz:
Whether your organization is large or small – whether you are a corporate executive or entrepreneur – ask yourself these two questions:

1) _Are you outsourcing "artistry" as well as artisanship?_
    Many companies are eager to ship out the "grunt work" -- but have a much more difficult time bringing in outsiders who could provide insight, vision and ideas that are out of the mainstream. Don't overlook your ability to acquire artistry from online providers like 99Designs.com and Upwork.com.
    (We outsourced the artistry of cover design through 99Designs. com for this book!)
2) _Are you backing the right productions?_
    The success or failure of a movie studio is primarily determined by the projects that they select to produce, and how those productions connect with the audience. If the movie is successful at the box office, the studio is in the chips. A string of failures will bring any studio down -- even those with respected histories like MGM or United Artists. For you and your organization, it might take a longer period, and may be less publicized, but focusing organizational resources on projects and productions that do not meet with swift audience approval will doom any organization.

• • •

Not just for the "big boys and girls"
Show business also teaches us there is great opportunity for smaller players.

The movie, _Paranormal Activity_ was made for $15,000 – and earned about $200 million at the box office. A 2003 film, _Open Water_ about a couple stranded in the ocean as sharks are closing in on them, cost about

$130,000 to produce. It was shot around the schedules of the actors and other independent crew members. It earned $55 million in global receipts.

Two young schoolmates from the Boston area wrote a screenplay they wanted to make as a small film. The result was that Matt Damon and Ben Affleck – later to become more famous as actors than writers -- won an "Oscar ®" for writing their movie, *Good Will Hunting*.

The point here is that, just like in all businesses, the power of ideas can often compensate for the lack of size. No matter how large or well-funded your business might be, the principles we will discuss here can have a major impact upon your success in the future.

• • •

Show Biz Quiz
If you are with a smaller organization, here are three questions for you (even though these are important for a company of any size):

1) *Have you invested enough in original thinking and creative ideas to offset your larger competition's financial advantages?*
For example, several years ago, Intuit's Quicken and Quick Books products defeated the enormous resources of Microsoft and others in the field of personal and small business financial software. They did it with superior creativity and execution.

In today's world, there are a myriad of examples – from Facebook to Spanx – of successful companies that were founded with little more than a tiny bit of capital and a creative, original idea. Yes, innovative thinking and creativity are amazingly, breathtakingly difficult. Yet, these corporate examples – just like the success of the aforementioned independent movies – proves that the power of an idea superbly executed can defeat the industry Goliaths.
2) *Have you "panned for the gold" in your old ideas and practices (organizationally and individually)?*

Please do not believe for a second that this book is about throwing away all your established, yet persuasive, ways of doing business during this revolution we are discussing.

Yet, if your career – or your organization, department or team – is not as distinctive as you would like, you are not going to get there by working harder on a tired, old plan.

• • •

* **You need a new way of thinking – or, at least a new metaphor for understanding.**

Taking a fresh look through new eyes at old ideas can lead you to a smashing success.

For a show business example, think of a film close to my heart, *Hoosiers*. (The story is based in a town much like the one where I was raised in Indiana.) Here's an old film that was old fashioned...and was a huge hit. *Hoosiers* took longstanding ideas and made them fresh through the intense emotional connection the audience felt with the characters.

Look at some of your more established practices. Then, ask yourself how you can creatively alter them to update, upgrade, and enhance the emotional connections you are making with colleagues, customers, and prospects.

3) *Is your distribution as thorough as the "big players?"*
    Even though some of the aforementioned films came from small studios, they all had mass distribution. Surround your magnificent ideas -- no matter how small your pocketbook -- with a distribution channel that will enable all your prospects to see, touch and experience your products and services. The playing field has never been more level! The Internet provides customers the ability to access your products and services on a global basis. Your challenge is

to use the "show business principles" we will be discussing here to stand out in a crowded marketplace.

Even another example...

When you examine how movies are produced, you will find that show business is cutting edge. Frequently, movies are multi-million dollar corporations formed for intentionally short life-spans.

Companies around the world place a great deal of importance on a product's lifecycle. Another relatively new phenomenon is the short amount of time that many business endeavors are now given to succeed. In business today, if you do not make it quickly, you may not be given much of chance to make it at all.

Movies realize that the initial "shelf-life" of their product is probably going to be relatively short. It is an important aspect of the planning and the marketing that goes into the production of the film.

Film company executives understand that, in most cases, a significant portion of the success and notoriety of their product will be based upon the box office receipts of the first weekend of release. There are so many movies in today's marketplace competing for the attention of the audience, if your film doesn't capture both mindshare and marketshare upon release, you are in trouble. Waiting to fill the screens of movie theatres around the world -- and take your place -- are even *more* films...some produced from multi-million dollar investments...and other, low budget endeavors financed on the credit cards of the filmmakers.

Your business is probably not going to receive numerous opportunities from prospective customers to create emotional connections. Just as in the film industry, making some kind of immediate impact, or raising instant interest, is going to be critical to your success.

How you deliver that connectivity that bonds your customer to you must take place on a variety of "stages." One point of performance will be when they are in contact with you in person -- perhaps a visit to a brick and mortar store or on a sales call. However, it's also via Social Media of all kinds, on your website, and more.

If you can't establish connectivity – given the reality of the number of options available to customers in almost every market segment – they will just move on to someone who can.

• • •

Show Biz Quiz
On the top of a sheet of paper, write the words "emotional connections."

*   Next, divide the sheet vertically into two equal parts.
    a. On the left half, write the word "organization" at the top of the page.
    b. On the top right side, write your name.
*   Now, start thinking about the emotions that your organization arouses in its "audience."
    a. Make a list of the emotions that your organization provokes in its customers and prospects in the left-hand column.
*   Next, make a list of the emotions that _you_ personally stimulate in your customers and colleagues on the right side of the page, under your name.
*   _**IMPORTANT POINT! If you cannot think of any emotions that you or your organization arouses, then you have a lot of work to do!_

If you _are_ able to delineate several emotions on each side of the page, take a moment to review your list…then, ask yourself:

*   "Are these the _appropriate_ emotions required to create customers for life and energized, loyal colleagues?"

• • •

Chapter 3

● ● ●

Putting the Show Business Philosophy to Work for You

There are many steps that you need to take to move your business into one that adopts and adheres to the philosophy of "ALL Business is Show Business!" While the rest of this book will focus on specific approaches, let's get started with a few general concepts around which you can build experiences in your communication with customers to create more distinctive and compelling experiences.

Making your communication persuasive

Both entertainment companies and organizations committed to the "show biz" approach understand that there is a vast difference between being "effective" and "persuasive."

I have seen many newsletters, books, blogs, articles -- and more -- about becoming a more "effective" executive, manager, or company. And, all *should* become as effective and efficient as possible.

However, we (as customers and employees) want to deal with organizations and professionals that are persuasive, dynamic, and amazing!

Your business communication must shift from being "effective" to being "persuasive." Show business understands that the only way to get you to spend money on a movie is to *persuade* you to go to the theatre and dole out your hard-earned cash.

* An *effective* advertisement is one that tells you merely what the movie is about – but it does not necessarily move you to get up and go to the theatre.
* A *persuasive* advertisement generates word-of-mouth, gets people talking about the product -- *and* gets the seat of your pants into the seat of your local theatre.
  o It creates an emotional bonding between the movie (the product) and the audience (the customer).

The critical element in persuasion is the <u>emotional connection</u> between the "persuader" and the "persuadee"!

Yet, here are what many organizations and professionals clearly lack:

* an understanding of the fundamental need for emotional connections in business –
  o and the knowledge of how to create them.

As previously mentioned, these connections will now be generated on various "stages." Perhaps some will be in person – undoubtedly, a variety will be on social media of all kinds, on your website, and more.

In a former time in show business, actors traditionally stayed within one or two areas of their craft. For example, major movie stars rarely appeared as a main character on television series – and the public viewed doing so as a sign of a decline in the actor's career. Broadway artists considered themselves as master thespians, and would seldom venture to Hollywood.

Today, however, it's not unusual at all to see a major film star appearing in multiple venues. Let's use the example of Oscar ®-winning actor Matthew McConaughey. Consider McConaughey's recent career: He wins Best Actor for *Dallas Buyers Club*, wins accolades for his performance on

HBO's *True Detective* on television, and appears in commercials for Lincoln automobiles. (Quite successfully, in fact. According to the *Hollywood Reporter,* overall sales for Lincoln increased 25% just one month after the ads debuted.)

Previously, that simultaneous variety and constant exposure in an actor's career would not have happened in show business.

The same is true with your business. It's not enough to give a great performance when you are physically in front of your customer. You must deliver compelling communication on social media, on the phone, on the web, in your emails…and more!

Your customers are demanding more from you – on more "stages," on more platforms than ever before.

An entrepreneurial problem

Many independent businesses are based upon the specific skills and interests of the entrepreneur who founded the enterprise.

In other words – with apologies in advance for the stereotypes in the examples, but these are two that I know from personal experience -- some guy uses his welding skills out in his backyard to make a trailer to haul equipment. Then, someone else asks him to make another one. He is asked for another, then another, and suddenly he finds himself in the trailer business.

A woman bakes cupcakes that are so delicious, her friends and neighbors ask for more. Because of the demand, she creates a plan to turn her passion into a business. Now, she's making money selling gourmet cupcakes based upon her recipe.

The problem for these entrepreneurs (as it is for most) is that he is not a businessperson; he is a trailer person. She has an interest in the profit of her business – but her primary passion is her cupcakes.

As their respective endeavors expand, these entrepreneurs are often faced with a critical problem:

* Product quality alone is not sufficient. It might have sold the first several trailers or cupcakes, but now the business needs customer relationships and emotional bonding.
  o Unfortunately, these are frequently the precise skills that the entrepreneur has not been educated or trained to deliver.

The "show biz" experience in a business suit

As I watched the luggage carousel spin around long after the last bag had been removed, I knew I was in trouble. A brokerage firm in Norfolk, Virginia, had asked me to speak at an event for their high net worth clients. However, since the meeting was a Monday luncheon, I had traveled across the country on a Sunday afternoon in a pair of jeans and a sweatshirt. As I grasped the thought that my suitcase was nowhere to be found, I realized this was *not* the proper attire to address a meeting of multi-millionaires.

The woman at the airline baggage claim was cheery. "Don't worry," she told me, "we have another flight from Atlanta first thing tomorrow morning. Your bag will surely be on that flight." Equipping me with a small shaving kit of necessities, I departed for my hotel.

The next morning, right on time, I was once again strategically stationed by the baggage carousel -- and, once again, discovered that my luggage and I were evidently on separate itineraries.

I was met with the same cheery response. "There's one more flight in an hour -- it should be on that one!"

Keeping to myself the thought that the bag *should* have been on the plane *with me*, I anxiously awaited the next arrival from Atlanta. And, once again, I was disappointed.

Now I was at a point of desperation. A room full of folks worth seven figures and more were going to convene in an hour and a half to hear me speak -- and I needed a suit!

Dashing to my rental car, an old television commercial for Men's Wearhouse and their founder, George Zimmer, popped into my head.

If you're unfamiliar with the chain, it is a men's clothing retailer that was founded by Zimmer in 1973. Now it is a publicly traded company that has recently acquired one of its biggest competitors, Jos. A. Bank Clothiers.

Although no longer with the company, Zimmer became famous in the United States for his numerous television commercials that were frequently broadcast and that always concluded his closing phrase, "I guarantee it."

I called from my mobile phone and connected with their downtown Norfolk store. A woman with a wonderfully pleasant voice answered -- only to hear me immediately stammer that I needed help.

"I have a speech in less than ninety minutes and my luggage has been lost. I need a suit, shirt, ties, shoes, underwear -- everything! And I need to walk out of your store in an hour. Can you do it?"

Without hesitation, she immediately responded -- just like the store's founder in his old commercials that I remembered -- "Sir, I guarantee it!"

Wow! Notice at this point, if Men's Wearhouse can do what she and the store's founder have claimed, they aren't merely excellent -- they are *distinctive*!

She said, "Sir, the only thing I need to know are your sizes -- suit, shirt, shoes and so forth. We'll be ready." I gave her the requested information and sped to the store.

Sprinting in the front door, a well-dressed man standing next to a short woman said, "You must be Mr. McKain."

Wiping the perspiration from my forehead with the sleeve of my sweat-shirt, I smiled and asked, "What was your first clue?"

I noticed he had two suits lying side-by-side, with shirts and ties strate-gically placed inside them. Both were great looking outfits.

"I didn't know if a navy suit or a charcoal suit would best compliment your current wardrobe, so I wanted to show you each in your size," he told me. The tiny woman next to him was introduced as the store's tailor. As soon as I could try things on, she would start altering the pants so that I could depart the store at the necessary time.

The service was nothing short of astonishing. I even bought an extra blazer that could go with the pants of my new charcoal suit in case the lug-gage remained missing an extra day. The suit, shirt, tie -- even socks and shoes -- were of the highest quality.

In fact, I should admit that I had never shopped Men's Wearhouse before because I assumed the clothes there were not of the style I could find, for example, at a fine department store like Nordstrom. I was wrong. The materials and selection rivals just about any men's department. However, the service at Men's Wearhouse makes an emotional connection that keeps customers like me coming back.

When I arrived *on time* for my speech, I smiled as I walked into the conference room. You see, I received a couple of compliments on my suit! When it came time for my presentation, I began with the story of the local Men's Wearhouse.

Three points illustrate why this is important to the "ALL Business is Show Business" philosophy that we are discussing in this book:

1. **Excellence isn't enough in today's business culture.**
    a. I expect every store that sells men's clothes to have suits that will fit me, as well as a satisfying line of accessories. The amazing experience I received at Men's Wearhouse is what separated them from the pack of competitors in my view. This works for clothes, trailers, cupcakes – and your business, as well.
2. **Amazed customers cannot wait to tell others about their experiences.**
    a. I told several millionaires that very day. And, I'm telling you right now! This book will help you craft amazing experiences that will earn you the kind of "standing ovation" response I am giving Men's Wearhouse. There's no better way to build your business than have your customers help you.
3. **Men's Wearhouse had never received any of my money prior to this experience because they had never connected with me on an emotional basis.**
    a. It is important to note that emotional connections always precede economic ones in today's business culture. When they fulfilled my emotional needs -- not merely my product requirements -- they created not only a customer, but also a fan.

This works across the board

By the way, this philosophy works with your "internal customers" -- employees --as powerfully as it does with your external customers. Many employees that I've talked to over the years will state that they would quit where they are currently working and take a position with another organization if it was "more fun" to work elsewhere -- as an aforementioned research study supports.

The atmosphere of enjoyment becomes incredibly important for these employees. Your business is show business because *both* your customers and your employees expect to enjoy the experience of the relationship that they have with you.

Especially when considering the Millennial generation, you must be asking:

* Will these employees continue to choose to work for your organization?
* Will the customers that you seek continue to be your customer in the future?

Customers no longer want to be just "served." They want an experience! Employees no longer want a "job." They want to be thrilled!

The evolution in the thinking of best-selling author Tom Peters is a perfect example of this phenomenon. This business guru moved from being "in search of excellence" to – as the title of a later book emphasized -- in "pursuit of WOW!"

We live in a time when "great" isn't good enough to grow your business. As mentioned earlier, I explored in detail in *Create Distinction,* that the vast majority of the eleven "great" companies cited in the classic best-selling business book, *Good to Great,* are now performing at or below the average in the marketplace. The list includes one that has gone bankrupt and another delisted by the New York Stock Exchange and cited with securities fraud.

    *   **Just because your organization or your product is "great" today is no guarantee it will be superior in the marketplace of the future.**

However, when you create a powerful and compelling experience for your customer – with Apple being a primary example, as touted in the first edition of this book (well prior to the company's incredible resurgence) – you can achieve enduring success and profitability.

How do you use this philosophy when you create a product?

How a product is created is another way in which show business can be quite instructive on how we should manage our businesses.

Steven Spielberg is certainly a master at this, as the development of the film *Jurassic Park* and its sequels (*The Lost World: Jurassic Park*, *Jurassic Park 3*, and *Jurassic World*) clearly demonstrate. Show business icons realize that their customer -- the audience -- purchases an "experience." They know you are buying much *more* than what you might initially view as the "product."

If Spielberg thought the product he was making was solely the film, you would have never seen all the enormously popular merchandising and licensed products that the *Jurassic Park* franchise generated. Filmmakers understand that they must evaluate the audience quite precisely to be able to produce a total experience that generates maximum revenues through both the initial and ancillary products.

This is a five-step process:

1. *The initial product*
2. *The customer is purchasing the experience – not merely the product*
3. *Repeat business is fundamental to sustained profitability*
4. *Constantly seek strategies to entice the customer to upgrade the sale*
5. *One of your most profitable tools is the sequel*

#1) *The initial product.* How does the initial product (in other words the film, the television show, the book or the play) play to its target audience?

One of the reasons your business *is* show business is that you need to view your product as a *production.*

* *How does your product or service "play" to <u>your</u> potential audience?*
    o *Have you precisely defined your potential audience?*
        ▪ *(By the way, anyone with "a check that will clear" is not defined accurately enough!)*

If you do not know who you are "playing" for, the chances are good that you are not going to connect with your audience.

Imagine if you were putting on a play that is highly irreverent, erotic, and controversial -- and then find that your audience is a group of religious clergy! Imagine "Sponge Bob Square Pants" performing inside a maximum-security correctional facility!

Obviously, these examples are absurd.

* ***However, it serves the point that if you do not know your audience, you cannot be a success.***

Evaluate your initial product and service -- or management techniques -- against the standard of how it meets the demands of the audience for whom you are seeking to "perform."

Let's imagine, for example, that you are a financial consultant. This means that you should gear the investment instruments that you are recommending to the specific needs of each individual prospect. It is vital to note that the investment (just like a movie) must meet the emotional needs – not solely the financial needs -- of your customers and prospects to achieve client retention and long-term success.

Do not base your product decisions exclusively on demographics. A zip code-based marketing program in today's world merely means you are targeting people who have chosen to spend a similar amount for their dwellings. It tells you little about how they might FEEL about the products and services you offer.

#2) *The second way your business is like show business is that filmmakers are constantly trying to find additional products that allow the audience to purchase the "experience" created by the film.*
This is the reason we saw so many *Jurassic Park* lunch pails, notebooks, bed sheets, action figures, yo-yos and more! Later in this book, we will discuss how expanding your market -- and your audience -- leads to additional profits. For now, remember that one of the ways we need to emulate the show business model is by continually asking the question: "What are other additional products and services we can offer that will allow our audience to continue to purchase our 'experience?'"

#3) *Repeat business is fundamental to profitability.*
The reason *Titanic* became the biggest box office hit of all time (until *Avatar* came along from the same director), is the number of repeat customers it secured. Even though the movie lasted well over three hours, people wanted to see the film again and again.

As stated earlier, filmmakers look for additional ways for the audience to purchase the "experience" generated by the emotion of the movie through licensed products. And, they seek to develop a product that (in show business parlance) has "legs."

A movie with "legs" is a film that has a longer than usual "shelf life" at the box office. It is the kind of movie that attracts repeat business. It brings people in to see the movie not only once, but repeatedly.

A listing of all the top hits in the history of film -- from *Star Wars* to *E.T.,* from *The Avengers* to the *Shrek* series, to Matt Damon's latest as Jason Bourne -- clearly establishes that the key to enormous profitability is found in obtaining repeat customers.

Isn't the same thing true in your business? For every business I consult or speak for, the real key to earnings is in the *repeat customer.*

If you are an accountant, for example, the lifeblood of profitability is not a family for whom you prepare their taxes once and then never see again. It is in doing bookkeeping, advising, consulting, and tax preparation for your clients year after year after year.

A successful, small movie illustrates the point. *Memento* is the story of a man trying to track down his wife's killer. So far, that sounds like a pretty standard thriller, doesn't it? The plot device that makes *Memento* remarkable is that the leading character has no short-term memory. The screenwriter/director of the film tells the story backwards! It starts at the conclusion and the script works its way back to the beginning of the mystery.

A reason for this plot device is so the audience does not know more about events than the leading character – we are almost as confused as he. When you do get to the twist at the end – which, of course, is actually the beginning of the event that the movie is about (confused?) – the first thing you want to do is see the movie again, armed with all the information you now possess.

(The old film, *The Sixth Sense* was another that had a twist ending that drove the audience back to see the movie again. It, too, was hugely successful. The same filmmaker, M. Night Shyamalan, scored a big hit in early 2017 with *Spilt* – that also featured a surprise in the end...as the credits were rolling...that would stimulate the desire of the audience to see even more!)

Memento is a highly successful film because it is emotionally powerful and because it is structured in a way that makes us want to repeat the experience.

In addition, this 2001 movie introduced an audience to director and writer Christopher Nolan. He went on with larger budgets to deliver even bigger box office giants such as the "Dark Knight trilogy" of Batman films, as well as the hit movies, *Inception* and *Interstellar*.

An important part of the reason you need to align your business with the "show business" philosophy is because your organization must examine in these changing times how you can create an "audience experience" that your customers and employees will want to repeat.

#4) *The fourth area in which your business should become a "show business" is to follow the example used by movie studios: always look for approaches to upgrade the sale.*
Take notice of the many ancillary products now created by show business. From home video to pay-per-view, from the creation of DVDs to streaming a movie on your laptop or tablet, studios are always seeking modes to persuade the customer to upgrade the sale.

This is different from the merchandised goods and licensed products discussed earlier. (I doubt that we are ever going to see *Memento* lunch boxes and action figures! However, it worked perfectly for the later "Batman" films, made by the same director.) The "goods and products" side is there to persuade you to purchase *additional* items related to the initial product. This aspect may not relevant to all businesses.

"Upgrading" means we try to get you to invest more -- _after_ *you have already purchased the initial product.*

In other words, the question the movie studio asks is, "Once we get you to buy a ticket to the movie...how could we find additional ways to get you to pay more for that *same product?*"

Part of the answer for your business is to find new methods of delivery. Sometimes these avenues may surprise you.

The major movie studios fought the development of the VCR (video cassette recorder) many years ago, reasoning that if people could videotape a movie from the television – or could buy a video cassette of a popular film – why would they go to the theatre and purchase a ticket?

We know they were exactly wrong. Instead of sounding a death knell for going to the theatre, it instead created a massive revenue stream previously unavailable.

In many cases, you should embrace these new opportunities for distribution – and exploit them for your benefit.

Even show business organizations can miss the mark here. Contrast the movie industry that eventually leveraged the technological advancement to grow their business...versus recording companies that would still prefer that you purchase a CD of your favorite artist's songs, rather than stream them on services like Spotify and YouTube.

The movie studios are as strong as ever – while the recording company labels are swiftly sliding into irrelevancy.

> *   **Are there new ways you can deliver your product or service to your customers so that they will pay more even after they have initially purchased from you?**

The software business has this down pat. Once you have purchased something from Microsoft, you can be assured that you are going to be contacted later to buy an upgrade. This process seems to be repeated, each time with a new version offering expanded features and benefits.

This approach created a new area of thought in economics. While the "law of diminishing return" has been taught as a primary principle in understanding business finance, there are many leading economists (initially at the Santa Fe Institute in Santa Fe, New Mexico) discussing the "law of *increasing* returns."

It was enormously expensive for Microsoft to develop the code for a product like PowerPoint. Now, however, each sale creates increasing returns because the cost of the download of the product by the customer is negligible. (It's even less expensive now than when the program was packaged with CDs or DVDs with printed instructions.)

Add additional revenues to Microsoft from each product upgrade over your lifetime use of the product, or the monthly fees charged for a subscription to Microsoft Office. You'll find that PowerPoint becomes *more* valuable -- instead of diminishing -- the longer it is in the marketplace.

Organizations are also finding it advantageous to partner with specialized collaborators to increase and enhance revenue. Amazon's Echo and "Alexa" interactive intelligence becomes of greater value the more services it can provide the end user. If all your Echo did was let you order from

Amazon – or even control your Fire TV – it might be a good piece of equipment to own. When you add the ability to turn your lights on and off, control your thermostat, open your garage doors, order an Uber, do your banking, get a pizza delivered, listen to your favorite music, find a local plumber, track your fitness, and monitor your baby's activities – well, it becomes a practically indispensable device! The more you are able to do with your Echo (as a result of Amazon's efforts as well as their partnerships), the more the device increases in value to both Amazon and its customers.

Notice that many movies now come out on DVD or download in two versions. One is an exact copy of the "theatrical release" -- the other a longer "director's cut" version. Many videos will advertise that they contain additional scenes not found in the original film. DVD makes possible the introduction of many upgrades and features that were previously unavailable. For example, one recent DVD from Martin Scorsese featured his comments about the making of the scene on one channel that you could listen to as you were watching the movie on the other stereo channel.

In other words, you can now upgrade your movie purchase into a "guided tour" of the film from the director who made the movie!

Here are three questions you need to ask yourself about your organization:

1) If I become a customer who is amazed and thrilled by your product or service, how do you entice me to spend *more* money on that product?
2) What up-sells, enhancements, and upgrades can I purchase that will allow me to gain a more complete experience?
3) Are there collaborators or partners that I should be working with to help my product or service grow in value?

#5) The fifth way your business is in "show business" -- in every business endeavor one of the most profitable tools is the sequel.
I don't know about you, but if they make *Forrest Gump 2*, I am going to be in the theatre. I want to see what happens next to good old Forrest. If they find a way to do a *Titanic* sequel, millions of people will be there.

(By the way, what could the follow-up possibly be? Yet, since the original generated something like a BILLION dollars in revenue, you can bet the great minds of Hollywood would love to find a way to make it happen!)

As we mentioned earlier, repeat business is the key. But, repeat business does not solely mean coming back for more and more and more. It also means finding a different way to carry your product, your service, your experience to the next level. The curiosity factor of the audience must not be overlooked.

Part of the reason that mysteries – from the classic "Whodunits" of Sherlock Holmes of novels from olden times …to today's serial killer murder mysteries -- have fascinated us is: we all want to see what happens *next*.

One of the great showbiz practitioners of this philosophy is Madonna. I cannot think of anyone who would say that Madonna is a great technical singer. Few, however, would dispute that she is a fascinating entertainer. By constantly remaking herself – in other words, by creating a sequel of her own image -- she keeps us interested in what she will do next, even as she is approaching her 60's.

Another example is the remarkable career of the late David Bowie. His first hit, "Space Oddity," was released in July 1969. He continued to produce new music up until his untimely death from cancer in 2016 at age 69. That longevity is remarkable for any business – and nothing short of extraordinary for an entertainer!

How interested are *your* customers in your next move?

● ● ●

Show Biz Quiz:
To close this chapter, please answer the following questions:

1. How does your initial product or service fit specifically into the wants, needs and desires of the audience for whom you want your performance to play?
   o In what ways do you "miss the boat?"

2. What additional avenues are you providing for your customers to buy into your "experience?"
   o For example, is your website simply amazing?
   o Do you have ancillary products that allow identification with your organization? (Imagine if there were no Nike tee-shirts, caps, exercise outfits, and on and on and on.)
3. What do you do to encourage your audience to repeat the experience of doing business with you? How do you reinforce that they are doing the "right thing" by doing business with you?
   o Please note, a mere "thank you" card is not nearly enough. Any business can do that! *You* are in "show business!"
4. How can your audience upgrade their purchase?
   o How are you set up so that customers who have already bought your product – and then have had repeated their business with you -- can take it to a higher level and upgrade the initial product?
5. What is the sequel? How do you show customers what happens next? How do you give them a chance to take the experience to the next level?
   o Remember, this is not just upgrading the product they already have - it is enhancing their experience with something new and different - yet somewhat familiar, as well.

● ● ●

Chapter 4

● ● ●

When Times Change, People Change

As a kid, I remember it was always a big deal for my family to eat at a drive-in restaurant. It was the late 1960's, and I would be in the back seat with my sister, Shelley, while my mother and father were in the front seat.

In the Post-War 1940's, America was enhancing its love affair with the automobile. As the nation was becoming more mobile, innovative entrepreneurs were frantically searching for ideas to capture the dollars in the wallets and purses of these new travelers. Local restaurants either added a drive-in component to their existing diner, or established new businesses that enabled customers to eat inside their vehicles.

"The custom of 'driving in' for a charcoal broiled hot dog, hamburger, sandwich or fish fry became a popular alternative to the traditional sit-down restaurant," writes Mark Graczyk in *The Daily News* from Batavia, New York, in an article about the history of local establishments in that part of the country.

Dad would take us down to Cliff's Drive-In in Scottsburg, Indiana. He would pull into a parking space and -- believe it or not -- *park*! Dad would then roll down the window of the car (this was prior to power windows!) and place our order via the revolutionary technology of the two-way speaker system the restaurant had installed at each parking spot.

(I realize for many reading this passage and so familiar with drive-thru windows, this sounds like something from the Jurassic period.)

About five minutes later, here would come the "carhop" – the drive-in's version of a waitress. With a tray piled high with food, the carhop chomping on chewing gum -- sometimes she would even be on roller skates – she was heading straight for our car.

Dad would roll the driver's side window up a couple of inches so the tray would fit on the window. After we had the food dispensed and arguments about who had the most French fries resolved -- a strange conversation would occur.

Everyone inside the car would look at one another instantly before the meal would begin. Then, children and adults alike, all in the vehicle would exclaim, "Wow! We're eating *in the car!*"

In those days, it was forbidden to eat in the car. It was something that you absolutely did not do -- *unless* you were visiting the drive-in.

Times have changed. Now we do not drive-in, we drive *through*! We zip around the drive-thru lane -- and if more than three cars are ahead of us, we become impatient! Perhaps you are as time sensitive as I -- sometimes I don't want to wait on the drive-thru! I pull into McDonald's and shout to the order taker, "I don't even have time to *drink* the coffee! Just go ahead and spill it on my lap, and I'll keep going!"

With the advent of Uber-eats and other delivery services, we may even be rapidly approaching the point where driving through is too inconvenient. We will just say, "Alexa, here's what I would like for dinner" – and wait on its prompt arrival at our door!

Perhaps some older readers will remember when customers had to visit their bank on Friday afternoons to get enough cash in their pockets to make it through the weekend.

Long lines would snake through neighborhood financial institutions as people prepared for their Saturdays and Sundays. Regardless of the purpose of your visit or the specific nature of your transaction, the only way that you could conduct a banking matter was through a teller.

I am certain that banks thought they had reached the ultimate in customer convenience when drive-thru windows were installed at *their* institutions…just as they were at restaurants. Millions of banking customers probably felt the same way.

Now, of course, we do not stand in line for the bank teller to provide us with our needed cash -- we just swipe our card through an ATM!

At the time of their introduction, ATMs were equipment available only at banks. Now, as you know, they are a phenomenon found everywhere! From gas stations to hotel lobbies, from airports to casinos it seems you cannot go anywhere without running into an Automated Teller Machine.

Speaking at a convention in Las Vegas a while back, I saw a man in front of the ATM repeatedly inserting his card. He was just standing in front of the machine putting his card in, putting his card in, putting his card in. I asked him, "What are you doing?"

He replied, "It's the only machine in town that's *paying off*!"

ATMs have become such a part of the global landscape; we are seldom concerned anymore about how we will access cash. I am ashamed to admit it, but there are many times when I have boarded an airplane to travel across the country – or even around the world -- to present a seminar and realized I only have five US dollars in my wallet! The scary part is, it really doesn't worry me to leave home for a couple of weeks with little cash in my pocket. I know that I will be able to get money anywhere on the planet, anytime of day or night, from an ATM.

Amazing as it is to consider, cash itself is on the way out – meaning that ATMs are in danger of going the way of the VHS machine. With technology like Apple Pay or Google Wallet, we're now able to purchase what we want without cash in hand – or even our credit card – as long as we have our iPhone or Android!

The old "back fence" over which gossip and other information were exchanged is a thing of the past. The Internet, Facebook, and other forms of media have become the gossip and bad joke conduit of our times.

Do you recall the old television commercial where a young employee gets on an elevator in his corporate headquarters on the first floor -- and as the elevator ascends, various colleagues comment on a report that he has just e-mailed? At each succeeding floor, the people getting on the elevator remark about his report and how they have forwarded it on to someone higher up in the company. The young employee continues to receive promotions throughout the organization as his e-mail circulates and the elevator rises. By the time the commercial concludes, the corporate chairman on the top floor wants to see our young e-mail hero.

This television spot is obviously making fun of the speed at which business is conducted. Nonetheless, it makes a valid point that we now expect immediacy in just about everything we do.

What do these examples have to do with your customers? It means simply that, as the title of the chapter suggests, times have changed. However, along with those changing times, we must understand that *people* have changed as well. The buying behaviors of customers are impacted by the technological changes that have driven the speed of transactions.

Ric Duques – then the CEO of First Data Corporation until he led its acquisition by KKR for $29 billion in 2007 -- discussed the speed of electronic transactions as it pertained to the customers of First Data's well-known division, Western Union at a meeting where I as the keynote speaker.

First Data's basic mission then and now is to enable consumers and businesses to safely and securely pay anyone, anywhere, anytime. First Data is now a private company and is not required to report detailed results, as when it was publicly traded. However, at the time I was discussing this with Duques, he told me that Western Union served nearly 2.6 million merchant locations, 1,400 card issuers and millions of consumers – *instantly*!

Think about how quickly your credit card transaction is processed – or that you can wire money instantly to most places in the world. First Data understands that if you facilitate the speed at which transactions take place, you assist in creating more transactions.

Duques made clear during our conversation, however, that transactional speed is the mechanics of the business. However, he emphasized it is the *relationship* with the customers of all of First Union's divisions that are the *future* of its business.

"If we don't enhance the value of our relationships," he told me, "then customers won't value our ability to process their transactions."

> * *It is one of the most challenging conundrums in business today: How do we improve the speed of transactions...and the delivery of our products and services...while simultaneously enhancing and deepening the relationships we have with customers?*

Perhaps nothing describes how dramatically that times have changed -- in terms of speed -- as in the differences in how we watch television.

I remember the television set on our own farm. Dad constructed the antenna, and brought the TV into the living room.

Isn't it interesting to note that in the early days of television the most popular shows were the "variety shows"? In the 1950's and 1960's, Milton Berle, Red Skelton and, especially, Ed Sullivan dominated television with programs that featured something for everyone.

Now, television sets are no longer exclusively in the living rooms of America or homes around the world -- they are in every room in our homes! Dad might be in the den watching ESPN or Sky Sports. Mom may be elsewhere with Lifetime, Eve, Passion, Mya, or Nova – the network depends upon where she is in the world. You will probably find one child in a bedroom watching Nickelodeon, while another sibling is in their room absorbed in the latest reality show on MTV. One major change is that the television that used to bring us together as a family now separates us demographically *in our own homes.*

In the old days, we would watch a television program, and if there was nothing on the networks that was worth watching -- we would turn the television set off and wait thirty or sixty minutes until our favorite programs would appear.

Now -- how do we watch television?

Picture the man sitting in his recliner, pointing the remote control at the television set and going ZAP-ZAP-ZAP-ZAP!

If something good comes on the television, what does he do?

He keeps *changing* channels, for there might be something <u>better</u> on someplace else!

My wife tells me that the way she watches television is to sit on the couch while I zap through channels and say, *"What was that? What was that? What was that? What was that?"*

As famed comedian Jerry Seinfeld says, "I believe women want to know what is on television. I believe men want to know what *else* is on television."

My point in describing the changes in how we watch television -- as well as how we dine and bank -- is to detail something that should be pretty obvious: Times have changed. (Yes, I know that is not a remarkable statement. You already knew that.) However, I mention it to also illuminate an aspect that many have not yet grasped, perhaps precisely because it is so pronounced:

* **As times change, *people* change. These people are our customers.**

• • •

Show Biz Quiz

On a sheet of paper, answer the following questions:

* How can I repackage my personal style to appeal to differing demographic groups and generations, as television programs do?
* How do we need to change our products and services to attract customers and potential employees across a greater demographic and generational spectrum?

* Do we need to insert more of the "fun factor" to appeal to a generation raised on television?
* Consider this: Are the attention spans of your customers and employees getting shorter? If so, this is part of the proof that people are changing during these changing times. How have you changed your organization's communication style to address the shorter span of attention?
* Isn't it logical to assume that people
    o who are totally accustomed to driving-thru instead of driving-in
    o who go to an ATM instead of standing in line for a teller
    o who zap through channels incessantly
    o who have spent most of their entire life with products just one click away from home delivery
        ▪ -- bring a different set of expectations about the role of business than customers did just a few years ago?

• • •

Television — and its role on our businesses

Nielsen Media Research released a study that states the average American watches TV more than 5 hours every day. If you add the time that we are watching a television program, movie, or other program on our smartphone or tablet, we spend more time looking at a screen than at any time in history.

At this point, I know what you're thinking. You are probably saying to yourself, "Well, *I* don't watch that much television."

That is not the point. The point is that your customers and employees *DO!*

* **No matter how good your organization is at selling and serving -- no matter what your proficiency is in training and motivating -- you are not going to be able to overcome the**

"training" that people around the world are receiving from our extensive smartphone/tablet/television screen habits.

Let me emphasize – especially as a former television news anchor – that I do not believe that this dominant influence of television and the entertainment industry is the ideal situation. However, in business we must deal with situations the way they ARE in order to create the kind of returns that we want.

A front-page article in the *Wall Street Journal* told the story of Lynne Collier, a restaurant analyst for a brokerage firm in Little Rock. Her claim to fame was having great success in picking the right stocks for her clients.

What was the secret to Collier's success? If customers were willing to wait in line for an extended period to enjoy not just the food, but the *experience* of the restaurant, it was one in which she wanted her clients to invest.

P. F. Chang's, The Cheesecake Factory, and Outback Steakhouse are examples of restaurants she caught on the upswing. Seeing the decline in the waiting lines at other restaurants helped her get her clients out of stock positions before their corporate shares declined.

It begs the question – is your experience so compelling that customers are willing to wait to receive it? If not – you're in trouble!

Why would any organization be arrogant enough to assume that these customers or employees we have discussed – the ones driving through the restaurants, getting their cash from an ATM machine, zapping through cable or satellite channels, as well as streaming movies and television programs on demand on a daily basis -- would want to *wait* on anything from you?

There is only one reason: *a customer experience worth waiting for and savoring.*

*   *By the way, here is a thought to ponder: if the element that obtains and retains customers is an emotion-driven "show-biz" experience…is an MBA (as currently constructed) relevant in today's economy? If all your business training has evolved around economic (rather than emotional) principles, can you compete when the rules of the game change?*

The impact is powerful

See if you can complete the following sentences: "Winston tastes good like…"

Or, "You can take Salem out of the country but…"

If you are not able to complete those sentences, do not worry. It only indicates you are probably too young to remember, or are in a part of the world where these products were not advertised.

However, if you can complete those sentences that "Winston tastes good *like a cigarette should,*" and, "You can take Salem out of the country but *you can't take the country out of Salem,*" you have proven the power of television. Those commercials have not been on the air since 1972, yet many will still remember the messages.

My personal belief is that it is no coincidence that the first generation in the United States raised on television violence has turned out to be the most senselessly vicious American generation in history. We are tragically seeing the result of a violent media culture in places like Aurora, Colorado…Newtown, Connecticut…and Blacksburg, Virginia. It is relatively easy to predict the same for future generations.

You may disagree with this point. That is certainly your option – but please answer this question for me: If you do not think that the entertainment media has impact, why would your organization spend its resources to advertise?

The impact of our "show business" culture is dramatic – in many ways, both positive and negative.

We find value and power in…

Here is one of the most shocking words you can use in American business:

Emotion.

It seems that many times we are afraid to consider the emotional impact we have on our employees – as well as the emotional value our products and services bring to customers. Emotional involvement is a very real part of the value of the relationship an organization has with a customer or an employee.

The traditional focus of business strategy has typically revolved around *economic* principles: costs, growing market share, enhancing shareholder value, etc.

I believe that, given the cultural and behavioral changes in customers and employees that we have previously discussed, a significant portion of the focus of our business strategy must shift to *emotional* principles.

In business schools and corporate strategy sessions alike, much intellectual energy has been expended to create a satisfactory and all-encompassing definition of business.

The central principle here is that if we can define "business," we then might have an easier time establishing its central purpose. Simplistic definitions such as, "the purpose of a business is to make a profit," have been supplanted by more market-oriented definitions. For example, a market-centered definition would be: "the purpose of a business is to enhance its value to its shareholders, stake-holders and owners."

The business definition I prefer is one that has often been attributed to Peter Drucker -- although other management sophists have synthesized it and taken credit for it as well. This definition is *"the purpose of business is to obtain and retain customers profitably."*

It seems obvious that if any organization:

1. *obtains* customers -- in other words develops products, services and practices that employees execute with an approach that moves customers to <u>want</u> to do business with you
2. and *retains* those customers in a profitable manner

-- that business will become successful.

This definition needs to be taken at more than its face value.

*   *If obtaining and retaining customers is the very purpose -- by definition -- of business, we need to closely examine the elements that will allow us to do so in today's changing culture.*

We have said earlier that customers want (some would say "need") an emotional contact and relationship with an organization to remain loyal to its products and services.

We previously discussed those 70% of customers who would change where they do business if it was more "fun" elsewhere. These customers are obviously not feeling a strong connection where they are already doing business. So, why are they so fickle?

* *The missing element is neither product nor price -- it is an emotional connection.*

If we accept the previous definition of business, and we agree that emotion is one of the main (if not *the* main) elements required in today's culture to obtain and retain customers, why shouldn't we revolve our business strategy around it?

Is your only reason, "We have never done it that way before?" That is not good enough in today's changing culture!

* **In today's world of change, you cannot succeed by merely working harder on the old plan.**

Perhaps your organization – and you -- need a new plan!

Sometimes, we are so grounded in the past that we risk appearing irrelevant. At a recent business conference, the small talk just before getting down to the main issues revolved around the hit television show, *Empire*.

One of the people around the table remarked that he had absolutely no idea what we were talking about. He then proudly announced, "I *never* watch television. Don't have time."

His smug attitude delivering the statement revealed something about his personality. He thought his lack of knowledge about television gave him a point of superiority because he was too busy for something that he felt should be considered so trivial.

In fact, his remark had the opposite effect from the one he desired. "For God's sake," one of his colleagues remarked later, "how can you _not_ know what _Empire_ is? It's the number one show on television!"

"I mean," she said, "if our customers are all watching it – and our employees are all watching it – and he thinks that it is great that he doesn't – then, who is the one that is really wrong? He doesn't have to watch it every week, but how can you not even know about it? Who is the one out of touch with the real world?"

• • •

Show Biz Quiz:
Here are your questions:

* What is your favorite television show?
  o Why?
* Answer on a separate sheet of paper and we will examine this a little later in the chapter.

• • •

Rational manager meets emotional customer in the same person
It is amazing to me how some senior executives -- who scoff at the notion that emotion drives business -- become extremely passionate when they talk about _their_ customer experiences.

* _When they are viewing their own business, they become highly product oriented and analytical._
* _When they play the role of customer, they are just like everyone else._

I was discussing this point with a top executive at one of the nation's largest technology-driven companies. He was disagreeing with the concept of "show business". He said that for every company, the focus must be kept on economics and technology. However, he also commented on how he wanted to continue to share information with me and to perhaps bring me to lecture to his organization.

Then, he pulled a product that I recognized out of his coat pocket. It was a "pocket briefcase" from Levinger's, a mail order catalog house and retail outlet that specializes in "tools for serious readers."

I am a Levinger's fanatic. I have become hooked on buying fountain pens and all kinds of accessories from them -- including the pocket briefcase. I noted to the executive, "Oh, I see you shop at Levinger's too."

Immediately, his entire demeanor changed. His eyes rolled back into his head like a dying calf. His knees buckled, his body swooned.

"Oh man!" he exclaimed. "Are they the best, or what?" He went on, "When I receive their catalog, I just want to call up and say, 'Send me one of everything.'"

I told him I had the same feeling. I also told him how impressed I was with many things about their operation -- the knowledgeable way that their operators take orders over the phone, the way they can customize the nib of the pen to fit the style of your writing specifications, the quick manner in which orders are fulfilled and the wide variety of useful products that they sell.

"I feel exactly the same!" he said. "I think they are just the best! I really love doing business with them. I just can't get enough of Levinger's."

After he made this last comment, I couldn't resist asking a question. "What if," I inquired, "your customers felt the same way about *your* company?"

A long silence followed. "Oh, that could never happen in our business," he said.

"Why not?" I asked.

"Because customers just cannot feel that way about our type of business," he declared.

"Why not?" I asked again.

After much thought, the look on his face softened. It was as if you could see the light bulb go on over his head, just like the old cartoon cliché about someone finally having an idea or gaining understanding.

He smiled and said, "I see what you're saying."

Suddenly, he realized that he had assumed that customers could not feel that way about his product because of *his* focus on the technology -- the hard assets -- of what his company manufactured. It never occurred to him that customers could get emotional over the same product he approached from an analytical perspective.

* **I would ask you the same question: What if your customers felt the same way about your organization that you feel about some company that makes you a loyal, committed customer?**

What companies make you starry-eyed? Is it the service from Nordstrom's? Maybe it is the products at the Apple Store? Perhaps it is the wonderful car you drive from BMW?

Examine your purchases of the past year or so. Which ones have made you swoon?

Emotional response is the beginning!

In every successful show business endeavor, eliciting an emotional response from the audience is an integral part of the design of the product from the very beginning.

Naturally, there are several different emotional responses you may want to create. A comedy obviously seeks the response of laughter and fun. A drama may want to make you feel melancholy, angry or motivated.

I am suggesting that now, because you realize that your business is "show business," you begin with a clean slate. Begin thinking of how you will engineer the appropriate customer response at every step along the way. By focusing on emotion throughout the process, you begin to take the steps necessary to create the experience the customer will want to repeat.

* **In other words, strategies for show business success precisely mirror what organizations should be planning today:** *how do*

we create distinction in order to elicit the desired emotional response from the intended audience?

It probably goes without saying, but some companies -- just like some movies -- are going to be more effective at this than others. Exactly like any other aspect of any business, some will do it well...and some will not.

Let's take the example of one genre of entertainment that saw great success a few decades ago – and periodically has a resurgence in popularity. There is a very basic and standard premise to the classic genre called the Western.

It is the creative and strategic execution of the premise that determines the success or failure of the product. In film, this is primarily achieved through the ability of the director to lead her team of artistic and technical professionals to create a product that will elicit the desired emotional response from the audience. It is through the excellence in execution that we discern the difference between *High Noon* or *Unforgiven* -- versus *Heaven's Gate*.

ALL businesses are going to have to learn the basics to make powerful emotional connections happen for a very important reason: *The Future.*

In the first edition of this book, I made a prediction about the future of business. Please know I did not throw the idea out in a casual manner. I seldom make prognostications. I want to make certain the predictions that I do make are ones about which I feel 100% confident.

And, while the concept I advocated has yet to be fully realized, there have been changes in the past several years that have progressed us toward its fulfillment.

Here was my prediction: *"I believe,"* I wrote in 2001, *"that in just a few short years, we will not even be talking about 'customer service.' Customer service will seem as old fashioned and outdated as the bell-bottom pants and 'zoot suits' from previous eras. What visionary businesses will be trying to create rather than customer service is a fabulous 'customer experience.'"*

Obviously, this did not become true – although, I would suggest that we're talking infinitely more about the "customer experience" than we did back then. And, it is true that visionary businesses like Apple are more focused upon the experience than on mere service.

The prognostication hasn't been fully realized. Why? In part, because I never considered that so many businesses would remain so remarkably inferior at delivering service – therefore requiring that we would have to continue to talk about it!

It is simply a fact that people want to repeat pleasurable experiences and they want to avoid repeating disappointing ones. The big difference now is that in these media-centered times -- where your business is "show business" -- the customer is adding the element of *emotion* to their decision-making process.

* I am not merely reciting the old sales training line about "sell the sizzle with the steak."
* I am telling you that in these times of change, *the sizzle is an integral part of the steak!*
* You cannot separate the sizzle from the steak – and you must not separate the experience of the customer from the product or service your organization provides.

So how do you begin to build an amazing customer experience? There are three areas in which you will need to focus your strategies:

1. *Product*
2. *Service*
3. *Experience*

Product

* *How does your product go beyond mere "pleasing the customer" into customer amazement?*

Later in this book, we will be discussing the aspects that customers *really* want when they do business. Let it suffice for now to say that customer expectations have never been higher. They expect quality to be designed into your product. But how much have you tried to do the little "something extra" that causes an emotional connection with your product?

In the decade that I was seen throughout the world on television as a film critic, I often said the worst thing that you could say about a movie was to praise its photography.

The reason? If the photography is the aspect that you notice, it means the emotion of the story has not been conveyed. Certainly, lousy production values detract from any film.

Yet, the point of the movie is not for you to notice the lighting and set design. It is to convey the emotional impact of the story.

The design of many products is troubling at best. Dr. Ken Dychtwald, author of the bestselling book, *Age Wave* was the first I heard outline how absurd some product design is for an aging marketplace of Baby Boomers.

When I was originally writing that last paragraph fifteen years ago, I experienced a part of what Dr. Dychtwald was talking about. I was staying in a 5-star hotel in Dallas and working at my laptop when the telephone rang. A client for an upcoming presentation obtained the number of the hotel from my office and wanted to touch base on a couple of last minute details.

"By the way," she said, "I need to fax you a copy of the appearance agreement so you can sign it and return to our office."

"No problem," I respond, "the fax number here is…uh…hold on, I can't see it here on the phone…uh…"

The problem was *not* that the fax number wasn't on the telephone's dialing instructions. The problem was that some under-30 graphic designer with perfect eyesight had no idea how much difficultly a middle-aged hotel guest would have reading such small type! Have you ever squinted in the shower as you tried to determine which of the little bottles was "shampoo" and which was "conditioner"?

While most of us no longer have any use for fax machines, the moral of the story remains relevant. I will promise you that there will be many more professionals in their mid-40's and 50's staying at that hotel than graphics designers in their mid-20's. Yet, it seems as if no customer who will be using the product – in this case, hotel telephones or hair products in the show – is ever asked if there are ways to design the experience to make it more functional and emotionally appealing.

What I am suggesting to you is that customers now expect a high-quality product to be a part of their experience. A product cannot be so technically amazing that it is difficult for the customer to use.

On the other hand, a product cannot be so sloppily engineered that customers notice a lack of product quality as part of their customer experience.

It didn't matter how cheap the price was on a small car from Yugoslavia, the "Yugo," that was sold in the United States from 1975 to 1989. The car was of such an inferior quality that very few people were willing to seize the low cost because the product quality was so lacking that the experience was horrifically inferior. *Time* magazine called it, "The Mona Lisa of bad cars," and said it felt like something "assembled at gunpoint."

Even the lowest price in the industry won't save your business if the product creates such an inferior experience for customers.

Service

As you plan the creation of a unique customer experience, the way you serve that customer is obviously a part of the equation. When I predicted that the talk will be about "customer experiences" in the future -- rather than "customer service" -- I did not mean to imply that service would become passé. Instead, I am suggesting that customers are blending all parts of their experiences into a meaningful whole.

Service, unfortunately, has traditionally been thought of as something separate from the product. Many organizations that I have worked with over the last two decades completely divide those responsible for the product from those responsible for the service. That's insane!

When you attend a movie, the product (the film you are there to see) may be wonderful.

But,

* if the theatre is dirty
* if the popcorn at the concession stand is stale
* if the bulb on the projector is so old that the movie isn't as bright as it should be

-- well, you get the idea.

The "product" might be magnificently assembled, but if the service is not built into the customer experience, the customer simply is not going to be satisfied.

Notice, too, that we are saying that customers must be "amazed" and not merely satisfied to ensure loyalty. Customer service is an important piece of the equation for any customer -- even those who maintain that they are "price buyers."

Several years ago, in my home county in Indiana, a concerted effort was made to acquire a major economic development project. The goal was to attract a regional distribution center for Walmart.

An impactful story was related to me by a development executive who worked on the project. He was told during a visit to the Bentonville, Arkansas headquarters of the retailing giant that, in the initial days of Walmart, their goal was to be the primary choice for those customers who considered themselves to be "price buyers."

Under the guidance of the late Sam Walton, who founded the company, extensive research was done to determine exactly what segment of the marketplace considered themselves as "price buyers."

According to the story as related to me, the number that the research developed was 17%!

I have never been able to find independent verification of that story. However, let's just consider, for argument's sake, that it is fairly accurate.

*   *My guess is that if you would ask most salespeople to pick a number, they would estimate the percentage of price buyers at exactly the opposite - 83%!*

Nonetheless, after developing this statistic, as the story was told me, the Walton family concluded it was wrong.

Even for the 17% who predominantly identified themselves as "price buyers," if the Walmart:

*   was not clean
*   well lit
*   fully stocked
*   staffed with courteous employees

-- then, even those "price buyers" would go someplace else.

That is part of the reason that Walmart employed the "greeter" at the front of every store. The purpose was to let the customer see from the moment they walk into the door that the company recognizes that they are still in the business of service. (Even from a company with a slogan of "low prices every day.")

Experience

It took a long time for business leaders to get accustomed to the notion that customer service was every bit as much a part of the customer's decision-making process as the product.

Many companies still do not understand it. They may *say* that they do – but customers know different because of the experience that they are providing.

This is quite natural. It occurs mainly because we have spent so much time trying to develop a superior product. We are so proud of the technical aspects of the products we sell that we think like "manufacturers and marketers" rather than "customers and prospects."

* **The primary reason that thinking about the customer experience is so challenging is because it adds an additional layer on top of the non-technical aspects of our business – which is precisely where most professionals feel insecure.**

What is the customer "experience"?

Because of many reasons -- most notably the impact that the entertainment culture has had on our society -- customers are blending the facts about the quality of your product and the delivery of your service with the *feelings* that they have about the experience of doing business with you.

The customer often does not distinguish between fact and feeling. If they feel it strongly enough, the rationalization factor kicks in. In other words, customers will rationalize with "facts" (that may or may not be true) to justify the way they feel.

As the entertainment culture continues to dominate our society, this effect has become more pronounced.

Let's continue to use a show business phenomenon as the example: Why is the 2012 movie *The Avengers* one of the biggest films ever made in terms of box office receipts?

If you examine what has made the movie so successful, you will see that the filmmakers – from the studio (Disney), to producer Kevin Feige, to director/writer Joss Whedon -- followed the three steps we have discussed in this chapter.

First off, the product is phenomenal. The technical aspect of this film is without peer. The special effects are absolutely amazing. The performances from the cast are letter perfect. The screenplay, written by Whedon, is engineered as a perfectly structured product. In other words, what you see on the screen -- the product -- is of the highest caliber.

But, what is the "service" of the film? This can cover many areas. One might be the demand made by the producers of *The Avengers* about the qualifications of theatres in which the movie would play.

In the early days of the film's release, *The Avengers* had to be shown in only the "best" theatres. In other words, those theatres with the most sophisticated sound, projection, seating and so forth. The reason? The producers wanted to make certain that the service provided the customer was part of what was engineered into the product. They knew that you can make a grand film, but if you show it on a small screen with bad sound, you are not serving your customer.

I am certain it is also easy to assume that the theatres with the best projection and sound are also the ones that have the cleanest seats and best popcorn. All of these synergies contribute to the kind of customer service that producers want to establish.

However, it is in the area of experience, that the movie *The Avengers* excels. This is the key to why it was able to move from being a successful film -- a movie that was well made, well-acted and well displayed -- into one of the biggest box office hits of all time.

The genius of Joss Whedon in this film and others is his clear understanding that special effects and amazing story do not make a unique experience. Many movies have had great special effects but fail to live up to expectations.

Here's the point -- people do not naturally go to see movies about superheroes, superspies or shipwrecks. But people will go repeatedly if there is a connection -- an experience -- that moves them emotionally. The emotion that drives the film creates an emotional experience that makes this movie a classic.

Consider the former box office champion, *Titanic*, for a moment. When I read about the scores of people who died on the actual ship Titanic, I understand that fact intellectually. When it is portrayed through a compelling love story, I now connect with the incident emotionally.

A similar situation exists with the Civil War of the United States. I can read about the fatalities at the Battle of Vicksburg and memorize the statistics. Yet, when I read the story of one soldier trying to make it back home in the brilliant novel, *Cold Mountain* by Charles Frasier, I have a powerful emotional experience I will never forget.

• • •

* When customers connect with your **product**, they are *interested*.
* When customers connect with your **service**, they are *appreciative*.
* When customers connect with your **experience**, they are *amazed, loyal and want to repeat the experience you provide*.

• • •

This is a fundamental point: **Customers want to repeat experiences that positively impact them in an emotional manner.**

The key to the box office success of films like *The Avengers* – and its 2015 sequel, *Avengers: Age of Ultron* – which, as of mid-June 2015, had earned about $440 million -- is that many fans saw the movie multiple times.

The key to the box office success of all the Walt Disney animated classics is that people see the movies over and over again. They saw them as children -- and then they take their own children and feel the emotional connection anew.

This phenomenon also helps to explain why sports fans are so loyal. Even when the team they follow closely loses a game that they attend, the emotional connection with their favorite team drives them to repeat the experience.

There was a Monday night ritual for several years in the McKain household. My late wife, Sheri and her sister, Leslie, would watch the nighttime television soap opera *Melrose Place* together. The unique aspect was that Sheri and I were living in California, while Leslie lived in Florida.

The sisters would call each other during the commercial breaks and talk about what had just happened on the show. Obviously, the reason they did it was so they could immediately share the emotional experience of the program with one another.

I am not criticizing this! One of my best friends, Mark Mayfield a noted speaker and humorist, and I do the same thing during sporting events. During televised golf tournaments, we will call each other and say, "Can you believe that shot?" Even though we live over 1,500 miles apart, we have shared many sporting events because of our emotional connection to the games.

Have you ever seen a film where you just had to go to a coffee shop afterwards to talk about it? Why?

Even though we appreciated the product of the filmmaker and the service of the theater, we still must connect and share the *experience*.

  *   **That is another advantage of creating a customer experience that is amazing and astounding -- customers are driven to <u>share</u> their experiences.**

Why do we hang on to a stock long after we should have sold it? Why are we often filled with the hope that it just might come back? Is it economics?

I would suggest it is emotion.

Why do we go back to the dry cleaner who puts the crease in the wrong place but greets us cheerfully by our first name? Is it because the dry cleaner is cheapest -- or because we feel an emotional connection?

When we need the services of a funeral home, do we sit down immediately following the death of a loved one and comparison shop for the best value for our dollar? Or do we go to the establishment whose demonstration of genuine compassion touches our hearts?

Even if you have not planned what your customer's experience will be, you are sending one out. A bland experience for the customer will elicit no response, loyalty or word-of-mouth marketing. A negative customer experience develops a strong negative emotional response.

Customers cannot wait to repeat the negative experience -- except they will relive it in front of their friends, instead of at your business. Or, even worse for you, they will share it on social media for a potential audience of thousands – even millions!

They will make certain, through their negative testimonial marketing, that everyone they know -- and everyone they can contact through any means possible -- will hear about what a lousy time they have had doing business with you.

However, a highly positive customer experience generates loyal customers, repeat business and marketing of the highest value. Happy customers tell friends so that they can repeat the experience together. Friends want other friends to have positive experiences, so they will recommend your business.

So, how are you:

1. Delivering an experience that is so superior that your customers will want to share it with their friends?
2. Encouraging and facilitating your customers to share their superior experience on social media?

• • •

Show Biz Quiz
Here are five questions about the customer experience:

1. Have you ever tried to design the experience the customer will have with your organization from his or her first contact with you as precisely as you have tried to engineer a product?
2. How do service businesses move from service to customer experiences?
3. How accurately do you service the "feelings" about customers toward your organization?
4. Why would a customer want to have an experience with your business?
   a. How do you know?
5. Why would a customer want to repeat the experience they had in dealing with you?
   a. How do you know?

• • •

The changing customer...

It is important to note this is not meant merely to exult the value of television, movies, and other forms of entertainment. The real message is that the culture has made some dramatic shifts...and, therefore, people have, too.

What are some of the main changes in customer and employee behavior? The research and contemporary evaluations of customers at our company suggests these five primary shifts:

1. *They are more time sensitive*
2. *They are more demanding*
3. *They have higher expectations of product and service performance*
4. *They have different standards about consumer and employee loyalty than previous generations*
5. *They focus on feelings as much as product technology and service delivery*

Some of these dramatic changes will be discussed in this chapter. Others will be focused upon as we address the aspects of creating the kinds of experiences that customers and employees will want to repeat.

Two currencies for today's customer

In this --

* Order today and receive tomorrow from Amazon
* Get news immediately online – even as it happens from Social Media
* Share everything on Facebook world we live in today –
  o there is a new currency.

The currency that today's stressed out consumer and employee values most is not money – it is *time*!

It means that as people have changed -- so has the impact of your product. It not only has an economic-sensitive value; it also has a time-sensitive one. To develop the "show business" business, you must re-evaluate what your product truly is. The employees who manufacture, sell and distribute your products and services -- as well as the customers who buy and evaluate it -- have changed.

To repeat an earlier example, if you own a movie theater, you might feel that the product is the movie that comes from the studio and is digitally projected onto the screen in your Cineplex.

To the customer, your product is something completely different. It is the feelings – whether laughter or tears – evoked by the "movie" you are showing and the experience that is an integral part of going to the theatre.

If you are in telecommunications, for example, you may feel that the value of your product is found in the "pipeline" you possess. You may believe the value is found in the terminals, the connections and the networks of your system.

To the user/customer, it is something completely different. It is the information and resources coming down the line.

You must reconsider what your product truly is. Also, you must reconsider how your product impacts your customers and employees. Customers and employees are "trained" by the entertainment culture and advertising that an emotional response is important regarding products and services. Therefore, you must ask yourself how your organization is factoring emotion and time into your delivery system.

* **How are you succeeding in helping add value to the customer's time – as they spend their money on the value of your products or services?**

One of the most challenging aspects of show business is that you're often only as good as your last hit. We've seen everything from actors to musicians finding their careers faltering when they are unable to sustain the level of performance and success that they are delivering to their audience.

Your business is no different. If you fail to continue to innovate and deliver an extraordinary experience, your customers will just go elsewhere.

• • •

Show Biz Quiz

Earlier, you answered the question regarding your favorite television program. Now, think about how your answer may help describe what you are looking for when you are a customer.

* If you like a comedy, perhaps you're looking for fun and enjoyment because of the hectic pace of the world today.
* If a program like "Sports Center" on ESPN or watching CNN was your choice, it might be because of the time sensitivity discussed earlier – you like getting information quickly and concisely.
* If your answers involved dramas or reality shows, perhaps it is because you enjoy getting caught up in the lives of the characters on those shows – and evaluating their behavior against your own.
* The point here is that any organization, any manager, any front-line service person can find some way – do <u>something</u> – that will make it more fun, more time-efficient or more emotional for customers to do business with you.

• • •

We can clearly see now that as times have changed, people have changed. For example, as previously mentioned, customers are now more *time* sensitive than ever. Frequently, the *financial price* -- in other words, the savings of a few dollars – is not worth the *time price* -- the amount of time and effort expended to save the money.

On another sheet of paper, make a list of your favorite commercials.

* *It might be a beer commercial that is the current fad – or one like the brilliant Amazon spot featuring two religious men of differing faiths – or one of the old favorites from Alka-Seltzer's "I can't believe I ate the whole thing," to Wendy's "Where's the beef?"*
* *After you have listed your favorites, ask yourself why these commercials are so memorable and why they stand out from the literally thousands of messages with which we are bombarded every day.*

The reason is probably because the commercials you have chosen establish some kind of emotional bond through the stories they tell. This connection transcends mere product information.

The point here is that these emotional connections can be established in just thirty to sixty seconds! This means that you – yes, YOU! -- can create powerful feelings with your customers and colleagues during a short transaction or period of time.

The future of your organization – and you!

For years, we have heard business speakers repeatedly cite the "buggy whip" story. This cliché focuses on the assumption that the last company to make buggy whips probably manufactured the best buggy whips you could imagine. The problem was, as the story goes, people did not need buggy whips anymore after the invention of the automobile.

One of the problems I have with this story is that the focus is on an irrelevant product. A fact that needs to stand out in this story is that it was not just a change in product demand that caused the demise of buggy whip manufacturers. It was a remarkable change in the culture.

The current shift in culture is infinitely subtler than the move into mechanization. That is why so many companies fail to understand why their business must become "show business." They clearly understand technology has changed. They just do not seem to take that knowledge to the next logical conclusion.

John Nesbitt predicted in his classic 1982 book, *Megatrends,* that as we become more high tech, we will also develop a need to become more "high touch." We will need, in changing times, to feel a connection to a group.

There is no doubt we are seeing Nesbitt's prediction come true. The advent of Social Media has provided the conduit for us to develop relationships and "high touch" with people we have not personally met through "high tech" connections. One of the strategically important points that visionary organizations have realized is the value of their product, service and/ or employment is no longer just economic. It is also of emotional value -- it is relationship and information oriented.

This relationship value becomes economic value to your organization. Unfortunately, many companies and business leaders have found it easier to cut costs rather than deepen relationships with customers.

Any way to run an airline?

Airlines offer frequent flier programs to those who buy tickets on their flights. In addition, airlines enhance the recognition that their best customers receive to an elite level. Loyal customers are important to airlines – just as they are to every business. This is not only because the repetitive sale is vital, but also because these engaged customers are frequently purchasing fares with little advance notice and are paying higher fares than leisure travelers would.

Forbes ran a post by Adam Hartung entitled, *United: This Is Not 'Any Way to Run an Airline.'* It outlined why United had become the worst rated of all U.S. carriers.

Hartung wrote, "United's strategy, like many, many businesses today, is to constantly strive for better execution of an old, historical business model (in their case, hub-and-spoke flight operations) by hammering away at cutting costs."

(Does that sound to you like the futility of the previously mentioned, "working harder on the old plan"?)

United Airlines, for example, formerly offered their "1K" members (flyers who travel over 100,000 miles per year on the airline) a special room at major airports. They featured special handling agents who were there to assist in anything that the 1K flyers might need. These lounges were more business-oriented than United's Red Carpet Clubs, which are open to anyone who will pay for that service.

In a cost-cutting move (notice a trend here?) United eliminated this special benefit for its best customers.

> * **I wrote United a letter several years ago that asked one simple question: "Please tell me the last time that any company improved its business by cutting services to its most loyal customers?" The letter – and the question – remains unanswered.**

As a former 1K member for well over a decade, I hated to lose those wonderful benefits. If I was flying from Indianapolis to Orlando, I usually connected through United's hub at Chicago's O'Hare airport. While that made no geographic sense, it certainly made relationship sense. I did not want to lose my elite status with United Airlines.

However, when United devalued their experience for their most profitable and loyal customers, they lost my business.

On the other hand, Delta Airlines has made a concerted effort to improve the customer experience in a way that their competitors seem to overlook. As a result, I am now a "Diamond Medallion" flyer at Delta – the equivalent of 1K in Delta's SkyMiles program. Over the past few years, United has lost mid-six figures worth of business from me because they have delivered an inferior experience and failed to appreciate customer loyalty in these highly changing times. The business went, instead, to Delta.

In other words, "cost cutting" unintentionally became "customer cutting" for United.

Here's the simple difference: United is stuck in the old business model of "doing it the way we've always done it." Delta realizes that *all* business is show business. As times have changed...customers have changed...therefore, Delta has changed.

Which airline would you rather be?

• • •

Show Biz Quiz

* Make a list of "membership sales" or "subscription sales" businesses you have seen over the years -- i.e., "Time-Life" videos, "Book of the Month" club, online learning centers, etc.
* Make a list of other businesses in addition to the airlines that have "Frequent Buyer" clubs.
* What are you doing to develop a feeling of "membership" among your customers and colleagues? Make a list.
* If you cannot make a list for number three…you are not doing nearly enough!

• • •

Notice that two of the points of this chapter may sound contradictory:

* *We want more personal attention*
* *We have no time for personal contact*

At a presentation to the users of NEC's NEAX communications systems, one telecommunications professional told me that he had a request to make a seminar that his department was offering available by video conferencing. Professionals from one department in the company said that they could not afford to spend the time necessary to travel to the meeting.

The conference in question was a mere *twelve-minute walk* away!

When I asked why they wouldn't make the walk, the response was illuminating – "They believed that the information could be obtained via the

Internet as effectively as actually being there. They felt that the benefit to be gained from group learning was not as valuable as the extra twenty-four minutes spent in the office."

Is it worth the time investment to go to your store, when we can have it delivered by Amazon to the customer's door? Is it worth it to discuss my investments with you, when I can automate my portfolio online?

Don't misunderstand, you need to be connected with customers on-line, with a high priority given to mobile connectivity. However, whether it's in person – or via the Internet – are you creating such a compelling experience that today's customer will view their time with you as a good investment?

No matter whether it is a transaction of knowledge or groceries, you must find an approach to create powerful emotional connections even as you use technology to improve the speed of the transaction. Show business provides the model that you will require.

Changes in culture impact personal behavior

From restaurants to grocery stores, from banks to television, we have all observed dramatic and amazing organizational change. Often over-looked, however, is that these changes have not only influenced the culture. They have influenced the behavior of customers and employees, as well.

If we understand these changes about customers and employees – and if we acknowledge that they have changed – you must ask yourself this question:

* **Have you and your organization changed to meet the needs of these customers and employees?**

● ● ●

Show Biz Quiz

* List the ways you feel television has impacted our society in terms of customer behavior.
    o For example, are people more skeptical now because of the media?
    o Are they more demanding now because they are exposed to more options?
* Analyze the ways you have changed your business and/or product to relate to these changes.
* How have you made it quicker for customers to do business with you?
    o Are you more time sensitive in responding to customer and employee needs?
* Specifically, what new plans do you have to speed up customer and employee response while, at the same time, enhancing the relationships you have with customers and employees?

● ● ●

It is not about working harder. It is not even about working smarter.

* **It is about creating distinction in your marketplace.**

Remember, _in today's world of change, you cannot succeed by working harder on the old plan._

So…what are some of the elements of your new plan?

Chapter 5

Enhancing the Customer Experience

I hate to admit it -- especially when you consider that I fly about 200,000 miles a year -- but I am just a little bit of a fearful flyer. In fact, *USA Today* even published a lengthy story about my air travel anxiety on the cover of their Money section. The article discussed the many professionals who are required to fly for their jobs – and do so with more than a bit of trepidation.

No, I am not prone to screaming fits or terrifying nightmares about the experience of flying. It is just that I get just a little bit nervous when I get on a plane. The reason is not because of any particular fear of the way that a plane works, or the competency of the pilots. It is that when I buckle my seatbelt on an airline flight, I am giving up all control to other people.

Wanting Your Hands on the Wheel

Have you ever known someone who hated to be a passenger? When these people are riding in a car with you, do you observe their foot repeatedly pumping an imaginary brake? These people just hate to give up control.

I believe many customers are experiencing a similar anxiety today. They, too, want to have their "hands on the wheel."

Providing the customer with more authority and autonomy could be an important step to enhance the experience that our customer receives in this time of "show business."

One of the main buzzwords frequently mentioned in show business today is "interactivity." It's easy to see why this is the case when you consider these five examples:

1. *The interactive video game industry now creates higher revenues than the movie or the music business.*

2. *Pay-per-view movies and on-demand sporting events are now common.*

3. *Netflix, Hulu, and Amazon all provide the opportunity to watch both original programming and favorite movies and network television programs whenever you desire.*

4. *Several programs – such as WWE's global sports entertainment program, "Raw" – offer their viewers the "second screen" opportunity. Fans can sign on the WWE app, for example, and connect with other wrestling fans during the show. They even help decide stipulations and challengers for the matches on the live broadcast.*

   a. *Yes, I know that wrestling is scripted! (Sorry if you didn't know and that information spoils your experience!) This element of interactivity increases fan engagement and involvement. It's driving more subscriptions to the "WWE Network," an online-only television network that is a stand-alone, "over the top" channel not dependent upon inclusion by cable or satellite television providers.*

5. *Just about every television newscast now offers their viewers the opportunity to dial their "televote" line – or connect via social media -- to register your opinion. The reason this procedure works is that the interactive participant is an involved customer. That's an aspect that, arguably, started with show business.*

   * **This approach of prioritizing interactivity will work in *your* "show business," as well.**

The interactive customer can become so emotionally involved and connected to the experience your organization provides that -- when rewarded for their efforts -- they become more than customers. They also start working for you!

In other words, customers will begin to help market your products and services -- it's called, of course, "word of mouth advertising." And, customers will let you know how you can improve your product -- if you ask them for feedback in a manner that is emotionally satisfying.

Greatest Management Principle

"*G M P*" is the title of one of the best business books I have ever read. These initials stand for "Greatest Management Principle." The book has later been released in paperback under the title, *Getting Results.* Noted business writer Dr. Michael LeBoeuf is the author.

LeBoeuf is one of our most insightful business scholars – and, I am proud to say, a close friend of mine, as well. After reading his great works, including *How to Win Customers and Keep Them for Life,* I sought him out and found him to be as remarkable as his books.

* The "Greatest Management Principle," is so simple that it is deceptively powerful. It is: *"Behavior __Rewarded__ is Behavior __Repeated__."*

Bounce that sentence around in your mind a few times: "Behavior Rewarded is Behavior Repeated." It sounds simple, doesn't it? Yet, ask yourself -- how many times do we reward behavior that we do *not* want to see repeated?

Here's just one example: auto manufacturers offer rebates to such an extent that they have "trained" their customers not to buy a car unless discounts are offered. What began as a method to stimulate sales has instead become a way to create price buyers that erode margins and profitability.

Behavior rewarded is behavior repeated.

The question you need to be pondering is:

    *   **How can we reward our customers for doing business with us in a manner than both enhances their experience _and_ increases the likelihood that they will come back and do more business with us in the future?**

• • •

Show Biz Quiz
Four questions on rewarding what you desire –

1. What kind of behavior are you rewarding with your efforts?
2. What are your customers rewarded for doing?
   a. How about your employees?
      i. Have you even thought about it?
3. When a customer chooses you, what specific steps do you take to reward them for their good decision?
   a. Will they KNOW they have been rewarded?
4. When an employee comes to work, do you KNOW what actions they feel they are rewarded for doing?
   a. (Remember-- it is what THEY think that counts!)

• • •

The orientation of your business

It is easy for any business to become "product oriented." In business, we tend to fixate upon the technical aspects of the product or service we have created. This is natural. We have been trained for years to focus primarily on how our goods and services are engineered, manufactured and distributed.

When we study organizational behavior, we find that inside our companies we have also become highly "system oriented." Managers are frequently participating in intensive training sessions, retreats, and workshops covering how to develop and administer systems that enhance the efficiency of their organization.

The notoriety a few years ago regarding Six Sigma – in essence, a system that teaches how to improve systems and processes, particularly as promoted by then-GE Chairman Jack Welch -- is a great example.

One of the goals of Six Sigma is to eliminate variability. That's admirable in the manufacturing process.

* **Perhaps, however, we should consider Six Sigma a bit suspect when dealing with the aspects of every business that requires interpersonal relationships.**

Unfortunately, these areas of focus do not mirror what has been happening in society as a whole. We have already discovered that as a culture we have become much more "emotionally oriented." One of the challenges for any organization in trying to enhance their customers' experiences is that most of us are coming from a systems and/or product perspective. The customer, on the other hand, is often coming from an emotional perspective.

One of the ways in which you can combine the philosophies of the "Greatest Management Principle" by Dr. LeBoeuf with the ideas advanced in this book is to strive to create a "UCE."

UCE – Ultimate Customer Experience
UCE stands for *"Ultimate Customer Experience."*

* **What would comprise the *ultimate* experience that a customer could encounter in regards to your product or service?**
* **What would it take to move it from beyond mere "ordinary" to "extraordinary" to "*ultimate*"?**

One of the problems confronting fast food businesses like McDonald's and Burger King is that by their good works, they have "spoiled" their customer. By being consistent in providing fast food, what was remarkable when their companies were founded now seems pretty ordinary.

Utility companies face a similar -- and perhaps somewhat more severe -- problem in this regard. When was the last time you called the telephone company and said, "Thanks! My phone is working!"? If you're like me, the next time that I do it will be the first time I've ever done it.

The telephone service that was considered amazing a century ago is now taken for granted. The only time you notice the phone is when it does not work or your mobile phone drops a call.

In a way, too, this is a sad state of affairs, isn't it? You and your colleagues work diligently to create a product and service that is reliable, dependable, and of great value to your customers. Then, for your amazing efforts, you are rewarded with customers that are bored. That just doesn't seem fair.

* **The problem is that business - like *life* - isn't fair!**

Yes, it would be wonderful if customers recognized your efforts on their behalf. Customers, though, just keep raising the benchmark. When you are a customer, are you any different? When you drive through McDonald's, and they tell you that you must pull over and wait for your order, do you say, "No problem. In my business, I understand about unrealistic customer expectations?" No! You rev your motor to try to ensure the Big Mac gets there quicker.

In his classic book, *Real Time*, Regis McKenna – one of the early mentors of Steve Jobs -- states that we must prepare for "the age of the *never satisfied* customer."

Certainly, I agree with the premise that customers are getting harder to please. Yet, I would take an alternative approach. I would suggest customers simply must be amazed, astounded and thrilled. They must experience something close to a UCE -- or else we will lose their business!

Companies like Zappos, Nike, BMW, Starbucks, Disney, Apple, Lexus, and others can create it on an international level. Lesser-known companies are undoubtedly doing it locally or regionally in your area. So, why do we assume that customers will soon never be satisfied?

All it means is that we must keep raising the benchmark…as customers keep changing the game.

* **The problem is that – at least from my experience in working with hundreds of corporations of all sizes – many organizations have never even thought of what the ultimate customer experience might be!**

Organizations are so focused on the technical aspects of their product -- and the organizational politics within their business -- that the focus is internal rather than external. They display those behavior patterns that were mentioned earlier – a product and/or systems focus.

The adage that "most customer service is merely lip service" is frequently true. And, it is hard to even imagine the difficulties that an organization still focusing – and failing -- on customer service will encounter when the name of the game has changed to "customer experiences!"

Getting started on the UCE

As trite as it may sound, the first step to creating your organization's UCE is to start thinking about what it would entail.

* **Brainstorm with your colleagues throughout your entire organization about what the *Ultimate Customer Experience* would mean for your customers!**

A story I related in my book, "*Create Distinction,*" but bears repeating here as a UCE example, was something I discovered not long ago in Los Angeles. It taught me that even a business that has received a remarkable amount of publicity can decide to step up and deliver an Ultimate Customer Experience. We should not rest on the laurels gained from promotion and press releases.

For years, I have seen the multitude of pictures from the paparazzi of celebrities entering and departing famed Beverly Hills eatery, Spago. It was part of the reason I thought it would be a great place to take my wife to dinner for her birthday. This birthday was one of the "big ones," too, if you know what I mean. However, if I tell you WHICH one...she may not allow me to celebrate *any* with her in the future!

The timing was perfect! I had a speech at Pepperdine University with the legendary boxing champion George Foreman on Friday. My wife arrived in Los Angeles on Friday night -- and Saturday was her big day. I made reservations and hoped we would receive a great experience for her important milestone.

As we checked into our hotel, the desk clerk quietly informed me the special birthday plate of desserts that I had requested would be arriving from room service later that evening. Naturally, I kept that information a secret from my bride. We left the hotel to stroll Rodeo Drive and window shop before we headed for our dinner.

Then, only about ninety minutes before our reservation, it occurred to me I had messed up! I had completely forgotten to inform the restaurant of the special reason for our dining. I called Spago -- and they assured me not to worry, she would be cared for in a remarkable manner.

When we entered and I stated my name and reservation time, they acted as if we were frequent diners. (This was my third time there in about *fifteen years!*) Our gracious hostess escorted us to a fabulous booth, over-looking the entire restaurant. It was THE place to "see and be seen."

The risotto appetizer may be the best taste I have ever had in my mouth. Everything about the evening -- from the service to the food -- was nothing short of perfect. The small chocolate treat with a candle and "Happy Birthday" in icing on the side of the plate was an impeccable topping to the total experience.

And, there was a surprise for me was when the bill arrived. While certainly not inexpensive, we spent no more for our evening at Spago's in Beverly Hills than we would have dining at a top restaurant in our then-hometown of Indianapolis.

*   **Our evening at Spago was the Ultimate Customer Experience.**

The birthday plate to our room? *Never received it.*

I mentioned this to the front desk again as we checked out to be certain I wasn't billed for something I did not receive. They apologized, and a "customer relations manager" gave me her card and indicated they would send something to the room...the *next* time we stayed with them.

They totally missed the point. How many milestone birthdays does a husband get to provide for his wife? If they can't *get* it right this time – or, at least, try to *make* it right during our stay -- why would I ever entrust them with *repeat* business?

How has Wolfgang Puck remained on top in the extraordinarily competitive culinary world?

Here are three reasons:

1. *Deliver what you promise. Deliver <u>more</u> than you promise.*
2. *Treat everyone like a star -- even a couple from Indiana who won't ever have their picture taken by the paparazzi, but who <u>will</u> tell their friends, and return to be customers again when they have the opportunity.*
3. *Be so distinctive at what you do that your customers want to repeat their "show biz" Ultimate Customer Experience.*
   a. *And, they will tell their friends, so they will do business with you, too!*

By the way: are YOU *that* good?

If not...what does it take to attain that level of performance?

● ● ●

<u>Show Biz Quiz</u>

* Specifically, for your product or service, what would be the "UCE" (Ultimate Customer Experience)?
* When does it *begin* for the customer?

* When does the experience *end*?
* What does it look...sound...smell...feel like?
  o Remember – we want perfection! We want the ULTIMATE for your customer's experience!
* Write it down and discuss this with your colleagues – and customers!

• • •

Re-shoot, re-cast or re-edit

After a movie has been prepared for release, it is often shown to audiences at "test screenings" before it can be seen by the general public. Movie producers look for steps to improve and refine their films with these test screenings, much like internet marketers experiment on their approaches with "A/B tests," or like product marketers conduct focus groups.

Their effort to enhance the impact of their movie can provide us with insight into how we might refine the steps that we take in delivering the customer experience.

If there are glitches with the movie, they usually become clear because of the reaction – or lack thereof – by the audience. To fix the problem, the director and producers may decide to execute one or more of these three steps:

1. *re-shoot* some of the scenes
2. *re-cast* some of the actors playing characters in the film
3. *re-edit* the movie in a manner that makes the story clearer or enhances the emotional impact of the production

These same steps of re-shoot, re-cast, and re-edit from show business can help your business deliver the Ultimate Customer Experience to your audience.

Re-shoot

Perhaps your organization needs to "re-shoot" your product.

For example, Dole is in a conventional business – fruits and vegetables. Their position in such a traditional industry could create some marketing challenges. I mean, how many ways are there to advertise lettuce?

Changing the distribution channel is probably not a highly viable alternative. Most people are going to buy their lettuce at the supermarket, not order it from Amazon.

Dole, however, looked for ways to re-shoot the product – in other words, to find another way to create distinction and deliver an ultimate customer experience.

Recall the concept we highlighted earlier? The most important customer commodity is now *time*, rather than money.

So, Dole did a "re-shoot" of lettuce by dramatically changing how it was packaged and sold. Instead of forcing the consumer to buy a head of lettuce at their supermarket, Dole precut and pre-washed the lettuce and sealed it in easy-to-use packages. For the busy consumer, this meant an enormous savings in time. For Dole, it meant enhanced revenues and profit, as customers would pay more for a product that was more convenient.

• • •

Show Biz Quiz

* How can you "re-shoot" your product or service in a distinctive manner to create an ultimate customer experience?

• • •

Re-cast

To enhance customer experiences and improve customer perceptions, you may need to "re-cast" your employees.

The first thing that might come to mind when you read this is to make changes in your staff. I will not deny that in many organizations, this needs to take place.

As my friend Mike Jackson, a leading consultant in the vast industry of agriculture, states, "If you hire a dud and spend a lot of money to train him, you end up with a trained dud."

Jackson could not be more on-target! Many organizations have spent billions of dollars to train people who lack the fundamental skills necessary to execute their responsibilities.

* **Yes, "re-casting" could mean that you need to make changes in your staff.**

Yet, there is another definition for re-casting.

One of the steps you need to take in your business to make it a "show business" is to change the perception of the people who work for you.

For example, many organizations in the financial services industry have moved from the traditional view of salespeople into "trusted advisors" or "wealth management consultants."

While it may only sound like semantics, I can tell you from experience as a customer that I place a higher value on a "document workflow specialist" over that of a "copier salesperson." (Especially when that professional consults and advises me on my document management needs – rather than tries to manipulate me into purchasing a copier.)

Do not forget our earlier point – behavior rewarded is behavior repeated. When you reward marketing professionals for advising their clients rather than selling them – and even call them "advisors" -- you get enhanced customer experiences and relationships.

By calling them "advisors" you make abundantly clear to them you want them to advise and not just sell. Guess what happens next? They end up *selling more* -- because people want to invest more with advisors than salespeople!

Here is another one from personal experience: I would prefer to deal with a "mortgage consultant" rather than a "home loan processor."

Processing implies the customer is nothing than a number. An advisor (or consultant) is there to assist, advise and recommend the best alternative. Again, this serves to create a UCE.

An interesting part of this phenomenon is what psychologists call the "Pygmalion effect." This theory states that employees and customers -- in other words, *people* -- live up (or down) to the expectations established for them.

When you give an employee a title that implies the expectation of advice and consulting, your people tend to live up to those expectations. If their title is one of mere "processing," they will meet that low expectation for their performance.

* **Find approaches in your business to "re-cast" your employees in a manner that creates an enhanced customer experience.**

You can also "re-cast" your *customer* to improve the customer experience.

Don't get me wrong; I am not suggesting that you can tell your customer how to behave or how to perceive him or herself.

Instead, we need to look at our target customer and see how our business needs to change based upon how our customer has changed.

A great example of this is the customer of the resort destination company, Club Med. Years ago, many people thought of Club Med as being a place for "swingers." You know the type -- a few too many gold chains and just a little bit too "cool for the room" – frequently based upon their own evaluation of themselves.

One of the approaches that Club Med developed early in their organizational history was the concept that if you came to Club Med you were part of the "in crowd."

Club Med later faced an important realization. Those "swingers" who were their previous customers, now were people with kids and a mortgage! And, in this day of sexually transmitted diseases and more conservative values, Club Med was well on its way to becoming a demographic dinosaur.

What Club Med did was to re-cast the customer. Instead of being a place for singles, it changed its game – and several of its resorts -- into a haven for family vacationers.

The result is that Club Med remains a successful element of the vacation industry.

Is there any better example of re-casting the customer than my current home city of Las Vegas? Previously, Vegas focused on the "gambler." Now, they focus on persuading you to come have fun – whether you drop any money in a machine, on a table, or not wager at all!

It's amazing to me that gambling is *not* the biggest money maker on the famous Las Vegas Strip! "Since 1999, non-gaming revenue at the Strip casinos has exceeded gaming revenue," reports *Global Gaming Business Magazine.*

"Over the past decade, average per-visitor spend on dining on the Strip has grown by 29 percent -- nearly five times the gambling increase. Spending on shows and shopping is up 26 percent," writes David G. Schwartz, director of the University of Nevada Las Vegas Center for Gaming Research.

"And, if the slew of mega-club openings and six- and seven-figure DJ contracts didn't make it obvious, the biggest revenue winner over the past decade has been nightclubs: *The average spend per visitor is up by a whopping 60 percent.*" (emphasis mine)

Just as a movie studio recognizes the tastes of the audience may change over a period of time, Vegas realized that their potential customers were shifting in their preferences.

The younger demographic wants to party with famous DJs like Calvin Harris and Tiesto. Staying up all night playing blackjack doesn't hold the allure to Millennials as it did previous generations. So, Vegas had to re-cast its ideal customer from one that will sit and hit "deal" on the video poker machine…to one that is clubbing until dawn to the pulsing beat of EDM (electronic dance music).

Note, this also required a bit of re-shooting, as well. Floor space previously allotted to craps tables has now been converted to very upscale dance clubs and trendy restaurants.

Depending upon *your* situation, you may need to apply more than one of these three show business approaches.

• • •

<u>*Show Biz Quiz*</u>

* How can we re-cast our products and services to be more appealing?
* What do I need to do personally to re-cast <u>myself</u> to have greater impact?
  o Be honest.
  o Write it down.

• • •

Re-edit

Another way to create a UCE is to re-edit your distribution. In its early years, Disney viewed their business as the movie business. Now they distribute their characters through theme parks, licensed products and even Disney Stores in your local mall. By re-editing and enhancing their distribution channels, they have provided for enhanced customer experiences.

Your child is not required to watch a movie to enjoy the experience of Mickey Mouse. Now they can find it at the local mall. They even sponsor special "Collectors Showcase" days featuring seminars on their collectible products. Thousands of collectors will gather to purchase a specially numbered piece, meet the artist and just "hang around" the characters. The results are remarkable -- happier customers and happier shareholders!

* **How can you re-edit your distribution channel to enhance the experiences that your customers have -- to give them more "hands on" time with your products and services?**

At the relative dawn of the Internet era, Netscape re-edited the way the distribution was done on software products. They came up with a unique idea – "let's give it away *for free!*"

"Free" may not sound like a great way to make a profit. But, Netscape realized that by putting the product in the hands of the most customers possible, they would significantly enhance their ability to secure large corporate clients. As their user base grew because of their free distribution, so did their potential for enormous profits with additional products.

Today, we see many mobile apps for iPhone or Android that have a free, basic setup to get you to not just *try* their product…but, *use* it thoroughly. Many of the new users find they have more of a need for that particular app than originally anticipated. So, they move up to a paid-subscription or in-app purchase model that offers more features and customer support than the free version.

One of my favorite online tools is HootSuite – an app that allows you to schedule posts on Facebook and LinkedIn, and tweets on Twitter in advance. HootSuite is useful to help establish and grow a social media platform.

The more I used HootSuite, the more I wanted the additional features offered in the "professional version." The result was that I obtained a paid subscription. Now, I am even an official (unpaid) "evangelist" for HootSuite because I love the product so much.

In other words, HootSuite hooked me with "free" – and turned me into a loyal customer and raving fan.

• • •

Show Biz Quiz

* What re-edits need to be done in your organization?
* How about in your personal style?

• • •

Feedback and referrals

As you formulate your UCE and as you design your "show business" customer experience, you must design elements that encourage both feedback and referrals.

In show business, feedback comes from critics, audiences at plays, ratings on television, the box office on films and, in publishing, sales of the book. Feedback is easy to get in the field of show business.

It is probably tougher for your business. While it may be more difficult, it is just as important.

Moviegoers often choose which movie they will see on any given weekend based upon the feedback from critics in their newspaper or reviewers (like I was) on the local television stations. Other forms of feedback are vitally important as well. Word of mouth, noticing lines at theaters, and watching as people walk out of a movie are vitally important to any film's success. That is why movies often have "sneak previews." The studios will try to elicit as much feedback as possible to ascertain what changes they need to make in a product before its release to the general public.

What can you plan so you use the aforementioned "sneak preview" concept for your new products or services? How are you engineering the use of feedback as part of product development on an on-going basis?

* **You must find a way to create a system (the <u>business</u> approach) with the emotional response of your audience (the <u>customer</u> approach) in mind.**
* **To create the UCE you desire, product and service development must be ongoing.**
* **Remember the upgrade approach we covered earlier? Learning what your customers think and feel about your product or service is vitally important in this show business culture.**

The other aspect of this approach is to generate referrals. The feedback from local critics is often used by a movie studio as a referral to the potential audience to go see the film. What are you doing to generate referrals from your office? Does your website have a page that features referrals from users of your product or service? Are you finding a way to bring a systematic approach to word of mouth marketing in your organization?

• • •

Show Biz Quiz

* How can you develop a system that will enhance feedback and reward referrals?
* What are you doing personally to assist the process?

• • •

"UCE" meets "GMP"

Again, remember GMP. Put a system into place to <u>reward</u> those who refer you. Behavior rewarded _is_ behavior repeated -- so rewarded referrals create _additional_ referrals...and more customers who can enjoy the ultimate experience you create for them.

• • •

Show Biz Quiz
To close this chapter, answer these three questions once again:

1. Regarding our product or service, what is the ultimate customer experience?
2. What do we need to re-shoot, recast and reedit?
3. How can we develop a system that will enhance feedback and reward referrals?

• • •

Chapter 6

. . .

The "High Concept" Concept

Now that you have:

* *discovered that your business is a "show business"*
* *and explored how customers have changed*
* *and determined that they need to receive an "Ultimate Customer Experience"*

...we find that a critical question remains:

* ***How do you connect with your customers and employees during these crazy times?***

If you can't connect with your customers and employees, there's no way that you'll be able to communicate and establish those critical emotional connections with them. Once again, show business has the answer.

Let's start this chapter by playing a little game. I will give you a phrase that describes an old movie. Let's see if you recognize the movie being described in each of these three phrases:

1. *"Bomb on a bus"*
2. *"Shark attacks terrorize a small ocean community"*
3. *And a longer one..." A small group of soldiers must find the lone surviving son of a family and escort him safely home from World War II"*

If you knew any of these movies (and you probably knew all of them), you have just proven that the topic of this chapter -- the "High Concept" -- concept works!

Hollywood holds that you must grab the customer's attention in these channel-zapping, fast-paced times. You can connect with your audience by using the "High Concept" approach.

The "concept" of a movie, book or play tells you what that movie, book or play is all about. It describes, in some detail, the work of the author, director, playwright or screenwriter.

Because of the cultural phenomenon we've discussed, people today will not invest the time required to listen to a long, involved concept.

That is where the term – and the approach of – the "High Concept" came into being.

* **The High Concept is a short, powerful, attention-grabbing phrase that *interests* and *involves* your audience.**

When I mentioned the "Bomb on a Bus," you undoubtedly thought of the movie *Speed*. Even though it took you two hours to watch the movie – and it is over two decades old -- the High Concept allows you to explain it in a mere three seconds. ***That is powerful communication!***

The High Concept can even be as short as one word. Just the mere mention of the word *"Shark!"* evokes the image of the movie, *Jaws* – a movie so powerful in how it created an emotional connection in its audience ("fear" is an emotion!), that the film returned to theatres in 2015 to celebrate its 40th anniversary!

On June 21, 2015, over 500 movie theatres accustomed to showing the latest hits of Hollywood turned their screens over to a film that generated such a compelling audience response that people still want to see it on the "big screen" four decades later!

(Wouldn't it be fantastic to create a connection with your customers that is so emotionally powerful that they want to experience it forty years from the time you originated it? Whether it's the movies – or your business – that's the essence of success.)

The phrase about the soldier's journey is, of course, the high concept of another of the powerful movies of famed director Steven Spielberg: *Saving Private Ryan.*

Staying with old, classic films -- let's try one that is a little harder:

* *"Lone New York detective trapped in a Los Angeles skyscraper must rescue his wife, held in a group of hostages captured during a Christmas party by a terrorist."*

Did you guess the movie, *Die Hard*? If so, you are really good at this!

I mention that film to make this example: Once a High Concept is established, you may then build upon it.

* "Die Hard" -- *at the Airport – "Die Hard II"*
* "Die Hard" -- *without the Excitement – "Die Hard III!"*

See how it works? While that last one was a little joke…the fact remains that since the original in 1988, audiences have been thrilled with the adventures of that lone, smartass New York detective, John McClane, through *five* films – with, perhaps, a final installment entitled, "Die Hardest," yet to come.

(The other two were *Live Free or Die Hard* in 2007 and *A Good Day to Die Hard* in 2013.)

Visionary companies in today's "show business" times understand that this same principle works for their organizations, as well.

Here are a couple of old High Concepts used from a business perspective:

* *"Absolutely, positively overnight"*
* *"Your pizza in thirty minutes"*

Federal Express – now known through the abbreviated version, "FedEx" -- was basically founded upon its High Concept statement. Even though corporate decisions may involve millions of dollars or thousands of employees, the central guiding principle of FedEx is their High Concept. The most important question someone at FedEx can ask is, "How does this get help us move a package from one customer to another -- absolutely, positively overnight?"

To return to a theme from a previous chapter, as times change…people change. So do their demands.

Fortunately for FedEx, when businesses reduced their need to move documents overnight because of the proliferation of email and PDF attachments, it was precisely the time that companies like Amazon and a myriad of others were ramping up their need for the delivery of packages filled with products in short order. In other words, even as times changed – from the need to ship a contract overnight…to rapidly deliver anything from books to hairspray to shoes – the High Concept of FedEx continued to have traction with their customers.

You're familiar with some of the subsequent advertising campaigns for FedEx – "Be absolutely sure" …to "The world on time," for example. Later in this chapter, we'll address the difference between a marketing slogan and an organizational High Concept.

Domino's revolutionized the pizza business with their simple High Concept, "Your pizza in thirty minutes." While pizza delivery companies have been around almost as long as the pizza, Domino's use of the High Concept caught the attention of customers.

While the company hasn't guaranteed delivery in a half-hour since 1993, people still think of Domino's as the one to call for fast, to-your-door service.

As Snopes.com reports, "Domino's still offers its customers a guarantee that they will be satisfied with the product, but it is a quality guarantee rather than a time-dependent one. Says the company's Total Satisfaction Guarantee: 'If for any reason you are dissatisfied with your Domino's Pizza dining experience, we will re-make your pizza or refund your money.'"

Nonetheless, the power of the High Concept is proven – many of us still think first of Domino's when we want our pizza quickly delivered. However, there's another major pizza chain that comes to mind when we want a better tasting one.

The pizza business is an excellent example of a mature business that somehow creates innovative entrepreneurs who develop excellent High Concepts. My late wife, Sheri, used to talk about how she remembered a young man for whom she used to be the babysitter. She recalls him riding in her car, telling her that someday he was going to be the "President of a big company!"

While other little boys wanted to be firemen or baseball players, young John Schnatter had other ideas.

John – better known now as "Papa John" of pizza fame – had a great idea for a High Concept. "Better Ingredients. Better Pizza." Who wouldn't want to taste that?

These visionary companies understand that a customer or employee who spends most of their time at home zapping through channels and driving through restaurants is not going to have the time to listen to a long, drawn out explanation of what any organization does.

It is almost as if they have a remote control in their heads. If you go on too long about your organization, you will mentally get a *"Zap Zap Zap Zap Zap"* -- exactly like the channel changing on our television sets that we discussed earlier.

These organizations also understand that in today's world, customers and employees are looking for High Concepts. They do not have the time to listen to longer explanations, and with today's media-centered world, their attention spans simply do not allow it.

The Mission Statement Blues

This brings up an important, but controversial, point. **Customers do not respond to your mission statement!**

I cannot begin to count the number of companies with whom I have worked who have spent countless dollars and hours of staff time trying to craft the perfect mission statement for their organizations. Don't get me wrong. Mission statements are fine *internally* to ensure that everyone within the organization is "singing from the same sheet." (Although, honestly, even then I wonder if anyone reads them more than once in practical application.)

Where they are worthless is as a mode of customer connectivity or communication. **Customers do not care about your mission statement!**

Most mission statements try to include a little something for everyone. When you read most mission statements, it is easy to be reminded of the old joke that an elephant is just a horse assembled by a committee. For example, while it is important to promote diversity within your organization, there are few customers who will buy your product solely because of that. They assume in today's times that all enlightened organizations have policies to promote diversity in the workplace.

Another example: I do not ship a package by FedEx because of their commitment to developing a profitable return for their stakeholders! I ship FedEx because my package will arrive *absolutely, positively overnight!*

The High Concept of Southwest Airlines (yes, *another* Southwest example!) could potentially be described as "Cheap. Safe. Fun."

I do not tell my wife, "Come on, Honey! We're going to fly Southwest to enhance their shareholder value!" I fly Southwest for their High Concept. They are "cheap, safe and fun."

Notice this goes against what a company might perceive to be our human nature. For some reason, in business we have been trained to believe the *longer* an answer is – well, then the more *important* it must be.

When someone asks about your company, we tend to have a belief that the longer our answer is about what our company does, the more important and prestigious it makes our organization.

In fact, exactly the OPPOSITE is true. When the explanation is longer, we tune it out. When it is short and powerful – a High Concept – we respond!

Your personal High Concept

Every *individual* should have a High Concept statement, as well.

When someone asks the question, "What do you do?" Most of us respond with a litany of our responsibilities.

* *"What do I do? Well, let me tell you...I blah, blah, blah – on and on and on..."*

If we look closely, we see the listener's eyes glaze over. It has often become a joke, hasn't it? Some segments of business are renown for being particularly bad about producing people who just won't shut up when they start talking about their profession.

Larry Winget, a close friend and an extraordinary professional speaker, was constantly complaining that he couldn't get any reading done on airplanes because his seatmates would always talk throughout the entire flight about their careers.

So, Larry had a creative approach to the problem. He had a fake book cover printed. He would then remove the cover of whatever hardcover book he was reading and replace it with his own: *"How to Sell Life Insurance to People You Meet on Airplanes."*

He doesn't worry about interruptions anymore -- NO ONE from passengers, gate agents to flight attendants bother him when he travels because of the High Concept on the fake book cover!

While Larry Winget's example is humorous, the serious fact is that we each need a powerful, interesting High Concept statement that clearly describes what it is that we do.

(Do not become like the guy I met the other day. I asked him what he did, and his reply was, "There is a grand jury looking into it." That's a pitiful High Concept!)

The mutual fund division of a financial services giant retained me to speak on numerous occasions to the financial advisors at Merrill Lynch for several years running. Through these many engagements, I have met thousands of financial consultants. We have worked together with many of them to develop High Concepts that will help build their personal and professional success.

One of the most important aspects that we have learned through the Merrill Lynch experience about the High Concept is that it allows you to do exactly what an excellent High Concept does for a movie – *break through the clutter!*

Imagine you are both an executive and a lover of the game of golf. You receive many calls from financial planners who are seeking to invest at least a part of your portfolio. Then, one day a call comes in from someone who does not identify himself as a "financial consultant." Instead, he introduces himself as someone who will "help you raise your net worth – and lower your handicap."

That's an actual High Concept developed by a Merrill Lynch financial advisor from one of our sessions. My guess is that you will take that call!

Sometimes it's advertising...sometimes not

The best High Concept statements are incredibly difficult to craft -- but powerfully important to have.

Again, distinction is vital. Every business in the world would love to say, "Our High Concept is Exceptional Customer Service."

* *YAWN!*
* *Zap Zap Zap Zap!*

Who cares? That is a statement that is so generic that it is borderline sleep inducing. Unless your High Concept is interesting and involving, I will not listen to it!

High Concept statements sometimes *are* the advertising slogans of organizations. As mentioned earlier, FedEx is an example. "Absolutely, positively overnight" has become part of the national lexicon.

However, many are not advertising slogans or time sensitive guarantees. The Southwest Airlines, "Cheap. Safe. Fun" is not something they advertise -- it is something they exemplify by how they execute what they do.

Advertising or marketing slogans may serve you well as a High Concept. Yet, it's critical to understand that the High Concept statement is the essence of what creates distinction for your organization in the marketplace.

While your advertising may shift and alter to meet immediate marketing needs, the High Concept is usually much more enduring. An ad campaign may be brief, because it often describes a particular promotion or temporary sales push.

The High Concept describes the lifeblood of the unique culture and offerings of your company – and that should be something that has deep and lasting roots in your organization.

● ● ●

Show Biz Quiz

* Does your organization have a High Concept statement?
* Is it powerful…attention grabbing…differentiating?
   o Do you have an individual High Concept?

* Here is the most important point of all:
  o **If you cannot describe what your company does in a High Concept statement – how you are different and better than your competition – your <u>customer cannot either!</u>**

• • •

In my book, *Create Distinction*, I reported that the first "Cornerstone of Distinction" was "Clarity." The High Concept is an extraordinary tool to help you develop the clarity required to impact your marketplace. With it, you can be perceived as a unique, differentiated, and distinctive resource for customers.

Another Merrill Lynch example

Following a presentation to a group of beginning financial consultants with Merrill Lynch, I was asked by one of the attendees to review the High Concept statement he had prepared. It was: "I will help secure your financial future."

My response, "BORING!" Every financial consultant in America could make the same statement!

As we discussed the importance of distinction, he told me that he was in his second career. His first was his experience serving as an Air Force pilot. I told him to use *that* in his High Concept – it was something that could make him unique!

* *His High Concept now is: "I fly my clients through financial turbulence."*

This advisor sent me an e-mail to state that his business is up about forty percent in the past twelve months – despite significant market volatility.

He has taught me two important points about this concept:

1. *First; when you develop a High Concept, you make it possible for prospects who cannot remember your name to contact you --*
   a. When someone calls the Merrill Lynch office and asks for the guy who can "fly them through financial turbulence," the

receptionist knows which financial advisor they are asking for. It makes this financial advisor identifiable -- even if the caller cannot recall the name of the specific individual that he wants to contact.

2. *Next, when you develop a High Concept, you are writing your own referral script!*

   a. We want our clients to tell all their friends about *everything* our product or service can do. The problem is that the real world does not work that way. No friend is going to relate every point and attribute of your business to another friend during a normal conversation. (Do you talk that way to your friends? I'll bet it's not the case.)

   b. Friends *will* use a High Concept, however. They will say, "Hey, call this guy. He's flying me through all the financial turbulence!"

   c. With all the need for referrals in today's highly competitive marketplace, the High Concept can be a tremendous marketing tool.

• • •

Show Biz Quiz

* What is the High Concept of your favorite movie?
* Your favorite television show?
* Your favorite book?
* Think of the companies that are so good they knock you out --
  * What is their High Concept?

• • •

To get an even better idea of a High Concept, examine the back page of the "Life" section of any *USA Today*. You will see the television program listings there, including the movies being broadcast that day. From the classics to the worst of all time, they are each described by their short High Concept statement.

If they can create a concise, compelling High Concept for a multi-million-dollar movie that will take you two hours to watch, YOU can do it for your organization and yourself!

Developing YOUR High Concept

We have covered three points so far in this chapter:

1. *The definition of a High Concept*
2. *Why it is a significant part of show business communication; and,*
3. *Why it is so vitally important that your organization – and <u>you</u> -- develop such a statement.*

Now comes the hard part. Now it is time for *you* to focus upon how to develop *your* organizational and individual High Concept statement.

This is a process that, quite frankly, is a challenge to describe in a book.

Because it is impossible for me to know exactly what it is that you or your organization delivers in terms of your product or service, it is equally impossible for me to develop a specific High Concept statement for your unique situation.

> * **What we can do in this chapter, however, is to outline some of the <u>basic</u> steps that you need to take.**

In this way, you can create and craft a statement that will grab the attention of your customers, prospects and employees -- and interest them in what you and your organization is all about.

Three of the fundamental questions to consider in the development of a High Concept statement are:

1. *What makes your business (or you) different from your competition?*
2. *What makes you better than your competition?*
3. *What makes you and your organization unique?*

These are basic -- but vitally important -- questions to answer.

Many organizations are fighting the "price wars" without knowing why. If you cannot begin to define what makes you different, better and unique, then it is obvious that your *customer* cannot either. Therefore, they have no reason whatsoever to pay a premium for your products and services.

It's impossible for you to create distinction without extraordinarily clear answers to those previous questions. That's exactly why developing a High Concept is of critical importance.

Derivative -- but different.

Different does **not** necessarily mean "one of a kind" in show business.

And, strange as it may sound, in show business "unique" does not mean "being of a singular or sole quality."

It is not that I am trying to rewrite the dictionary; it is just that it is important for us to understand how the terminology is used in the entertainment industry.

One of the important principles in the show business industry is that a "sweet spot" where you frequently want to be is: derivative -- but *different.*

This sounds like an oxymoron, doesn't it? "Derivative -- but different." What this means is that all successful forms of show business derive from an inspiration that was probably generated elsewhere.

* *Part of the key to understanding the art of successful show business is to tap into previously established emotions and feelings -- and to put your own unique spin on the product or service so the audience perceives that your production is distinctive.*

For example, from the release of the first in its series in 1977, many fans have hailed *Star Wars* as a bold, visionary example of movie making. You will get no argument from me on that score. I truly believe that George Lucas is a modern-day genius. He fills the film screen with his vision much as a Michelangelo would use a chapel ceiling in historic times.

The on-going and lasting connection between audiences and fans of Star Wars is nothing short of amazing.

The original (which Lucas titled as "Episode IV"), to the sequels in the first series released in 1980 and 1983 – to the "prequel" trilogy in 1999 to 2005 – to the sequel trilogy which began in 2015 with *Star Wars: The Force Awakens* – to the spin-offs (the latest of which, *Rogue One*, has earned over a billion dollars at the box office as of this writing in 2017) – it seems that moviegoers around the world cannot get enough of this series.

The fact that is often overlooked is that *Star Wars* derives (in terms of its concept) from previous show business products.

Put the movie *High Noon* in outer space -- make Gary Cooper's sheriff into Mark Hamill's Luke Skywalker -- and you have a large part of what the movie is all about. Throw in a dash of the old Saturday afternoon serials -- especially "Buck Rogers" -- and you have *Star Wars*!

Is the fact that *Star Wars* is a somewhat derivative work a criticism of George Lucas? No! It is exactly the opposite! Part of the genius of Lucas is to create something that is different -- as *Star Wars* certainly was at the time of its release -- yet not _so_ different that it alienated (pardon the pun) the audience.

In another example, if you take *Godzilla* (which itself was released in updated versions in 1998 and 2014), add a slice of any movie about corporate greed – Hollywood fodder from *Citizen Kane* to *Wall Street* -- and you get the essence of the story of *Jurassic Park*.

By combining two successful concepts -- the ego of the mad corporate leader and the power of a prehistoric monster -- Michael Crichton created two bestselling novels, and the basis for several box office blockbusters. (It's a concept that has spawned several multi-million-dollar film sequels – remember that aspect from an earlier chapter?)

The point is to make certain you understand that when I say "different and unique," it should also be quite clear that it is permissible to be derivative in a sense as well.

To really stretch the thought, both Ferrari and Kia make automobiles. In that sense, they are both derivative from Henry Ford and beyond. Yet, it becomes quite apparent when you look at the cars (and especially the sticker price!) that they are quite different. How they exploit their uniqueness even as they sell the same product – a car -- will, in part, determine how persuasive they are as an organization.

High Concept vs. Unique Selling Proposition

Many of the "old style" sales training programs had a module about the "unique selling proposition."

Every salesperson was taught to clearly define for the customer what made their sales proposal exceptional. In those days, the "unique selling proposition" customarily focused on a specific feature or fact about the product.

Notice how in these "show business" times, this has a diminished degree of value. The customer is focusing less upon the facts about the products and more on their *experiences* in using your product or service -- and how they *feel* about dealing with you. Any primary focus on a technically related "unique selling proposition" frequently does not integrate with the cultural and demographic changes we have discussed earlier in the book.

To continue with the automobile example, Volvo has done a magnificent job of promoting their cars as safe. They do it by advocating that the technical innovations of the product mean that you and your loved ones will have a better chance of surviving an accident. The focus is not primarily on a feature like the air bag, for example. Every manufacturer has one, so its inclusion in a Volvo doesn't make them unique.

Volvo is marketing the unique *combination* of their features to create an emotional response that gives you the feeling that you are safer in a Volvo.

Volvo is not always rated as the top manufacturer in the government safety tests. But, I would wager that if you asked a prospective car buyer to associate a specific manufacturer with the word "safety," many would immediately say "Volvo."

We should note that sometimes *other* organizations could also fulfill the promise of <u>your</u> High Concept. It is just that if you are first to the marketplace and "own" the premise, your customers will view you as unique.

An example here is the FedEx "absolutely, positively overnight" High Concept. Other companies such as UPS and even the U.S. Postal Service are able and willing to deliver absolutely, positively overnight. But, FedEx was first in the marketplace with this High Concept -- therefore they "own" the franchise.

"First in" doesn't always win – but, it's not a bad place to be, either.

Methods for creating your High Concept

While there are many techniques you and your organization could use to develop a High Concept, here are two specific methods that may be of assistance:

Method #1

Start by examining your mission statement.

You may be surprised I am suggesting this, since earlier I stated that neither customers nor employees respond to your mission statement. The reason they don't is *not* because the information contained in the statement is inaccurate. It is ignored because of the *manner* in which the mission statement is presented.

Within your mission statement there probably exists some very important ideas, values and concepts about your organization.

* *Your job is to "mine the gold" out of your organization's mission statement.*

Begin by searching through your mission statement for the typical corporate clichés that cause your audience to "tune out." These phrases tend to talk in clichés about corporate niceties like "commitment to customers and employees."

While it is important for any organization to have these qualities, there is *no* organization that is going to say they are taking an opposite viewpoint! What organization could possibly say they are NOT committed to customers? Because comments of this type are so bland and generic, they constitute a "tune out" for your audience.

To revisit an earlier example, because of the values and integrity every company should have -- not to mention federal law -- FedEx, for example, had better have a diversity policy. I would choose to do business with someone else if I was aware that *any* company chose to disregard the importance of a diversity policy.

But that's a big distinction as opposed to why I choose to *ship packages* with FedEx, as opposed to the competition. I *assume* they have a diversity policy. I *assume* that they are committed to customers and employees. What I *really* want (as a customer) is to get my package to my customers "absolutely positively overnight."

A High Concept attracts me to do business with your organization, in part, because I assume everything else is in place. Your customers are making the same assumptions, as are your employees.

Continuing to "mine" the mission statement

As you continue to "mine the gold" from your mission statement, you may begin to develop the specific points that will make your organization stand out a bit from your competitors. This is the first step in determining what makes your organization unique.

Just like a committed prospector continues to search for gold no matter what he finds, you must continue to search through your mission statement. As you involve your colleagues in the process, you will find they will see different aspects than you do.

This is a powerful part of the process. You will glean different perspectives from these different ideas -- exactly as your customers and employees will.

Remember, the goal here is to continue to streamline and refine the mission statement. Do this until it becomes a short, compelling, and engaging High Concept statement.

Method #2
The second method of developing a High Concept is to brainstorm with colleagues about the key words that describe your organization. During this brainstorming process, it is important to follow a specific pattern. Here's a suggestion of a four-step action plan:

Step One: This is the "free association" step. Get your group to start shouting out words that describe the organization. Naturally, some of these will be humorous. Complaints about the organization will probably be cited, as well.

This is an important part of the process. People think more creatively when they are thinking humorously. Do not try to shut off the "fun valve" here. The laughter will open the gates of insight.

Another important point during step one is to make certain that *no evaluation of the ideas* takes place at this point. In other words, you just want people to be suggesting words – you don't want them evaluating the suggestions someone else has made during the exercise. At this step, we are looking for quantity not quality.

Step Two: Now that you have developed a "laundry list" of concepts about your organization, it is time to begin an evaluation phase. Try this three-step approach to improve and enhance the evaluation process:

1. Ask the individuals in your group to select the ten words that have the most impact on customers and employees -- as well as the ten that most accurately describe your organization and its strengths.

2. After the members of your group have individually made their selections, have them pair up and share their selections with someone else in the group. They should then, as a team, develop a list of ten.
3. Then, pair up the pairs -- in other words, create groups of four for your next discussions. Have these groups develop a list of only five concepts.

Notice what you are doing here is prioritizing the most important concepts, while at the same time ensuring that everyone in the process is being heard.

Step Three: After these groups have completed their work, take these five words from each group, put them on a flip chart and begin discussion. This is an interesting juncture in the process, as some groups are frequently surprised at what other groups believe to be important.

Try to narrow down these words to the two or three most powerful and dynamic aspects and qualities of your organization.

Then, create and craft a phrase that incorporates the concepts you have deemed most significant into your High Concept statement.

Step Four: One step that is fascinating to take next is to select a group of your customers (and, in some cases, *former* customers are a great idea). Involve them and proceed through the same process. Look at the disparities in the concepts that have been chosen.

You may find it fascinating that the qualities that are perceived to be most powerful internally are *not* the ones that your customers suggest. This would be vitally important information to have if you hope to craft a High Concept statement that has meaning to the people you want to purchase your product or service.

This should be an interactive and fun process for your customers or former customers. This is NOT a "focus group" to study the High Concept challenge – rather, *this is a time that you to "mine the gold" of your customer's insights.*

High Concept – DO IT, because you CAN!

Creating a High Concept statement is one of the most valuable communication tools that you and your organization can develop during these changing, "show business" times.

Don't forget that if you need ideas and inspiration on these statements, go to the television page of any newspaper and see how succinctly that classic films and shows are described in short High Concept statements. I guarantee if they can describe a $200 million movie in seven to ten words, you can do the same for your organization!

• • •

Show Biz Quiz

* What are the defining values of your organization? Are they outlined in your mission statement? Could they form the basis of your High Concept statement?
* Brainstorm a High Concept with your colleagues, then ask, "Are these the same thing our customers would say?"

Finally, here's a role-playing exercise:

* Ask your colleagues, "How are the responses we've given different from those that our competition would provide if asked the same questions about their products and services?"
   o If they are not different, you must ask…is your High Concept unique?
* Has your organization explored – and exploited – your uniqueness?

• • •

Chapter 7

. . .

The Power of Stories

The old man turned to me and said, "Son, where do you suppose that I got the money to start my first restaurant?"

I had never met the gentleman before, but I was familiar with him.

I was only twenty-one years old and was trying to make intelligent conversation with the famous man when he threw me a curve by asking the question.

I respectfully replied, "Well, sir, I suppose you had some money saved up."

"Nope," he said, "not a dime."

"Okay," I tried again, "did you round up some friends to become investors? "

"I didn't have any money -- and I didn't have any *friends* that had any money!"

"Did you take out a second mortgage on your house?"

He laughed. "Now, you're kidding me, aren't you?"

I laughed back. I didn't want him to know I hadn't been kidding.

"Give up?" he asked. I nodded. "My seed money to start my business was the entire sum of my first Social Security check. That's how it all got started."

Then Colonel Harlan Sanders continued to tell me the entire story behind the genesis of Kentucky Fried Chicken.

Two stories to start this chapter –

On this page and the next, I would like for you to read the following paragraphs, and then answer the questions on the third page to follow:

Story #1

The Ajax Widget is setting records for sales, and now we've lowered the price so you can have one of your own! Formerly 149.95, you can now have your very own Ajax Widget for only 119.95! That's a savings of thirty dollars!

Everybody ought to have one – and now we've made it affordable for you! With 18 megs of super power and 113 gigs that are guaranteed for five years, you cannot go wrong when you pick Ajax as the widget for you!

Story #2

It was a horrible night – cold and raining – when I got the call no father wants to hear. My little girl had been in an accident.

If you got that call…how would YOU feel?

No mother or father wants to hear that – but what we heard next was something we will be grateful for the rest of our lives. She was OK.

Why? Because the Ajax Widget had deployed – exactly as it was supposed to.

You know, I could've paid less. But, I can't help but wonder – if I would have…would she still be here? Get the Ajax Widget. Ask someone who has been there…

…and here's hoping YOU never get that call.

Question:

Now…without flipping back a couple of pages, answer these two questions:

1. *How many gigs does the Ajax Widget have?*
2. *How long is the guarantee?*

When I ask that question in seminars, most people don't know the answers because they cannot remember the information. Yet, the most important point to make is this: The ones that *do* remember, DON'T CARE! You don't want to buy an Ajax Widget because of its price or features – *especially* after you hear the second story.

* **Because of our entertainment culture, stories are more powerful than ever.**

We love hearing corporate mythology – remembering, of course that in academia, "mythology" doesn't necessarily mean that something is not true. It means the same as "legend" or "tradition."

We love hearing about how Hewlett Packard started in a garage. That same story inspires us about Jobs and Wozniak and Apple.

It could be argued that having a great story that creates emotional bonding with customers and employees was one of the ONLY attributes that kept Apple afloat during a tough period when they were trying to survive in a Windows-dominated world.

(Of course, Bill Gates' mother getting him the appointment that led to the licensing of MS-DOS is another great story.)

Southwest Airlines, in conjunction with a milestone anniversary, had several ads featuring its "mythology."

According to the story, cofounders Rollin King and Herb Kelleher got together and decided to start a different kind of airline. Southwest said, "They began with one simple notion: If you get your passengers to their destinations when they want to get there, on time, at the lowest possible fares, and make darn sure they have a good time doing it, people will fly your airline."

As the story is told by Southwest, King and Kelleher drew a triangle on a cocktail napkin. That shape represented the route map of the airline they had in mind, one that would begin by flying from Dallas to Houston to San Antonio.

Southwest is an airline that started with only three destinations -- and only three jets! Now, Southwest has more than 47,000 employees who serve more than 100 million customers annually. They now operate more than 3,600 flights a day, serving 94 destinations across the United States and six additional countries.

As you read this, many of you may be thinking, "Not another story about Southwest Airlines." I would gladly tell another carrier's narrative if one had circulated something as memorable as the story of how an airline started with just an idea and a drawing of a route map on a napkin.

> * **Having a "company story" is powerful and contributes to making an emotional connection with clients and colleagues.**

Did you know, for example, that United Airlines traces its history back to a flight by pilot Leon Cuddeback on April 6, 1926, for Walter T. Varney, who initiated airmail service over an isolated stretch of land between Pasco, Washington, and Elko, Nevada?

Didn't think so. I didn't either. But, it would make a great story -- if only someone would *tell it* in a powerful, engaging manner.

Can you tell me the genesis of US Airways? I can vaguely remember flying Allegheny Airlines when I was a kid. I recall Piedmont Airlines because they gave you the entire can of Coke. I know they formed elements of USAir – the company that became US Airways, and has now merged with American Airlines.

I know you won't have to guess which airline discussed here is more successful. Having a "company story" is powerful. It contributes to making an emotional connection with clients and colleagues.

*   **I am not saying it is the <u>only</u> reason by a long shot. But, ask yourself: do you identify more with the airline started on a cocktail napkin -- or the one that's a conglomeration of carriers you can't remember?**

Even though we love it when it comes to great movies and terrific television shows...and about other companies – our problem is that we seldom focus on *OUR* story...and how important it is for our business!

Storytelling – your most important skill?

The Futurist magazine is the leading publication for intellectuals who primarily focus upon future trends in the culture, published by the World Future Society. In an issue several years ago, they asked one of the leading futurists of the world, Rolf Jensen, director of the Copenhagen Institute for Futures Studies, to predict what would be the most important skill that a business could possess in the twenty-first century.

*   His answer? ***The ability to create and relate stories.***

As Jensen puts it, "The challenge will be for all kinds of companies -- whether producing consumables, necessities, luxuries, or services -- to *create the story behind their products*." (emphasis mine)

In the 1950's they asked a similar question for the second half of the 20th Century and basically the answer was: "the ability to understand and implement technical solutions." We can all attest that they hit the bullseye with that forecast.

For the next Century, the answer was, "the ability to create and relate stories." I agree! We are overwhelmed with technology today. We need to find some method to help make all the technical advances – and the products and services these advances have created – make sense.

Per the magazine, "If Jensen is right, companies will come to value storytellers not only in their creative advertising departments, but in executive positions, where refashioning a company's history and traditions into an appealing myth will be crucial for winning the enthusiasm of employees, the affection of customers, and the respect of the general public."

Somewhat later on the website of *The Futurist*, in a post titled "The Death of Brands," James Lee, founder of Strategic Foresight Investments, wrote: "Desirable products will have a history and narrative. The story could be about the artisan, where the materials were found, or how things were made. Successful niche merchandisers will be curators of unique products. Educated buyers are looking for full-disclosure on all aspects of their purchases, and demand far more detail than casual consumers."

That is the fundamental role of the story in business. *It creates the method by which our audiences (customers, prospects and colleagues) understand and emotionally bond with us, organizationally and individually.*

• • •

<u>Show Biz Quiz</u>

* What is the "story" of your company, department, organization, and team?
* How about YOUR personal and professional story?
* Write it out…then ask yourself:
    o What about this story is <u>compelling</u> for our audience?

• • •

Joseph Campbell and the Power of Myth

The most important – and frequently cited -- writer about the power of stories and myth is Joseph Campbell.

Author of several seminal texts, including *The Hero with a Thousand Faces* and *The Masks of God*, Campbell's work achieved significant notoriety as a result of a series of interviews of him conducted by Bill Moyers, titled *The Power of Myth,* that aired on PBS in the United States.

Campbell's work centers on the universal meaning found through narrative. His are perhaps the most significant texts available on how to craft compelling, emotionally connecting stories.

One of Campbell's primary points is that for the story to be compelling, the hero cannot begin the narrative as the winner. Only through trials and tribulations – being tested and defeated and then rising to conquer – do we have a hero.

* In Homer's *The Odyssey*, for example, Ulysses does not begin the book as a hero. It is through the experiences and difficulties that he faces that he becomes one.
* Consider the narrative told in the ancient New Testament. His followers recognize Jesus as divine through Christ's ability to endure and resist temptation.

The power of each of these works would be greatly diminished without the challenges that these heroes overcome.

Let's think about a couple of the "show business" examples we have previously explored:

* When Liam Neeson is introduced in the movie, *Taken,* he's not a hero – he's a divorced dad dealing with a decision regarding his daughter.
* As Bruce Willis enters the skyscraper in *Die Hard,* he isn't a hero. He is when he leaves it, though, because of the power of the story.
* Same thing with Keanu Reeves in *Speed.*

As a culture, we are "story junkies!" We get hooked on good stories! It can be scripted – as the "binge watching" that many of us do on Netflix demonstrates for millions of viewers daily. It can be "reality-based" – as *Survivor* and the glut of imitators are proving. Or, it can even be grounded in the business world!

I find it hysterical how many professionals tell me they don't watch television or follow anything like a "soap opera." Then, they cannot wait to turn on the television to follow the never-ending sagas on CNBC of *American Greed*…discover who is the latest to be charged by the SEC…or what's happening with Google or Apple's latest travails with the European Union…on and on.

Some will loudly proclaim, "That's different!" Is it?

With the proliferation of business television and 24-hour news channels, many political and corporate sagas today are depicted as something out of World Wrestling Entertainment…albeit with the leading characters wearing more distinguished attire.

As Jerold Duquette wrote, "Talk radio hosts are to political commentary and business analysis what pro wrestlers are to sports."

Whether it's politics, sports, professional wrestling, or *your* business – we are ALL in "show business!" Therefore, we must tell our story!

Tell YOUR story!

We *love* stories! And, if YOU don't take control of telling yours – and that of your organization – someone else will.

Nature abhors a vacuum.

So do customers, employees, the business press, pundits on Twitter, posters on Yelp, and gossips everywhere.

Your customers and colleagues want to know that there is a story – a compelling reason – about why it is that you do what you do…and how well that you do it.

* **If *you* aren't telling your story on the myriad of stages that we identified earlier, then you are abdicating control of your narrative to anyone with a laptop, tablet, or smartphone.**

This is important on a personal – as well as organizational – level.

* *Want to buy your new car from someone who is just selling them until something better comes along?*
  o *Or, would you prefer someone who is passionate and excited about automobiles?*
* *Should your stockbroker be a man who thinks it looks good on a resume?*
  o *Or, is your preference a woman who was inspired by investing at an early age and wants to help you learn what she knows as she facilitates building your portfolio?*

A great story inspires years of purchases

Over the past several years, I have purchased several new cars from Carl Nielsen at Dreyer and Reinbold BMW in Indianapolis.

The first time I was in the dealership, I was --- quite frankly -- not sold on BMW's. I was a Mercedes-Benz customer, and saw no reason to change. However, the BMW dealership isn't far away from the Mercedes one, and my wife encourage me to stop in.

Before we started looking at cars, and after seeing me drive up in my Mercedes, Carl said, "Let me tell you a little story." He started to tell me a story dating back to his days in high school. At first, I must admit that I thought, "What the hell does this have to do with me buying a car from you?"

Then, I realized he was telling me about his fascination with cars – and everything about them – from the time of his youth. He would tear apart engines; he would rebuild parts – it was evident that this man not only knew cars – he *loved* them!

He then told me, "Scott (I noticed that he remembered my name!), there are aspects about your Mercedes that are better than the BMW. But, I honestly believe that there are properties of the BMW that are so superior to what you are currently driving...well, give me a chance. I can prove to you that you should be driving one of my cars."

I have told people for years now that I am hooked on BMW's! But, before I could get hooked on the car – *Carl Nielsen had to hook me with his story!*

A final thought about Carl – I asked him a while ago if he could sell Mercedes, for example, as well as he could sell BMW.

"No," he quickly replied. "Look," he said, "I am a first-rate sales professional. I could use my sales skills for other products. I just couldn't be as successful because I wouldn't feel as passionate about anything else."

Most of the illustrations in this book have been about larger organizations – because they provide the most universally recognized examples to the most people. However, the development of your personal, professional and organizational story is something that every business – and every person – should be prepared to tell.

What makes a great story?

Whether it is a movie, television program, or your corporate story, certain basic elements are found in all stories, even though there are many ways to express what is important.

For example, in the book *How to Write and Sell Your Life Experiences*, Marjorie Holmes says the five fundamentals are:

1. *a provocative idea*
2. *appropriate style*
3. *smooth, sound structure*
4. *pertinent human anecdotes*
5. *a good clear summary or conclusion*

Kathleen Dinneen and Maryanne O'Connor of Yale-New Haven Teachers Institute conclude that good story writing should involve:

*   *the elements of character*
*   *setting*

* *plot*
* *point of view*
* *theme*

One of the most successful authors and lecturers on the subject is Bill Johnson. His book and seminar, *A Story Is a Promise*, suggest that a well-told story is both "a promise and a promise kept."

Johnson's point is that you keep your promise through the interaction of the elements of stories -- character, plot, theme, action, conflict, and resolution -- to create the effect of dramatic fulfillment.

Let's examine the elements that create a compelling business story.

The Hero

No company has ever started because all the customers in a given industry were thrilled, prices were low, service was high, and all was peaches and cream. Businesses get started because of some kind of challenge, problem, or need. When a business solves the problem, they become the hero, and a story is born.

There is no more frequently cited recent example of "business leader as hero" in our current popular culture than the late Steve Jobs. His founding of the business in a garage with a friend, being dismissed from the company he started, his return to take the organization from the brink of bankruptcy into the most innovative and highest valued company in the world -- before dying a young and untimely death -- sounds like a movie script.

(And, in fact, it *was* movie script – with at least two films on Jobs produced as of this writing.)

Consider your story -- or that of your organization -- for a moment. Have you considered who the "hero" of that story is? Could it be the founder of your company? Perhaps it's a sales professional who just landed a big account? It might become the customer service representative who saved a client and retained business that was going to leave the company. Maybe you want to consider developing stories that feature some of your customers as heroes!

Regardless of your choice, please remember that you cannot have a compelling story without someone playing the role of the hero.

Strong narrative tension

What would have happened if early in the movie *Speed*, Keanu Reeves had said, "Hey, no problem. We should be able to get everybody off the bus in about ten minutes. There is absolutely nothing to worry about"?

Well, you and I both know that if he had said that, there would be no hit movie called *Speed*.

Without the dramatic tension, we lose interest in the story.

We want to wonder what will happen next. We love to be thrilled by the hero's journey as he or she overcomes the odds. Many organizations do not pay enough attention to what happens in this part of the story. Remember Joseph Campbell's point: if there is no journey, there is no hero.

Note that the Steve Jobs narrative fits perfectly with the earlier point from Campbell – you cannot begin your story as a hero for it to have impact on the audience. Only through the ups and downs, the trials and tribulations does the Steve Jobs story have such resonance and reward.

To build this kind of dramatic tension, most novels, plays, and movies are written in the "three-act" format.

In a motion picture, you do not have an intermission between the acts, and the use of this format is seamless from the audience's perspective. In other words, the customers of the movie do not perceive the shift from one act to another, yet the film follows this format to build the audience's suspense.

ACT ONE

The first act is the "setup" or introduction. Here we are introduced to the characters with whom we will be spending the next couple of hours. We gain insight into what makes them tick. The first act is also where the fundamental conflict, question, or situation that must be resolved by the end of the movie is introduced.

To continue to use our examples from classic action movies, in *Die Hard*, for example, this is where we meet Bruce Willis's character and the hostages are taken in the skyscraper. Through the first act, the conflict is set up (what will happen to the hostages), and we meet and begin to identify with the main characters.

In *Speed*, the first act is where we meet the main characters, Keanu Reeves and Sandra Bullock, as well as the villain, Dennis Hopper. The bomb is on the bus and the nightmare for the passengers begins.

In the newer action thriller, *Taken*, the first act is where we meet divorced dad Liam Neeson, experience his discomfort with his teenaged daughter traveling to Europe, and witness her kidnapping. The first act closes with his memorable line to her kidnapper, "What I do have are a very particular set of skills; skills I have acquired over a very long career. Skills that make me a nightmare for people like you."

ACT TWO

The second act of the movie is always the longest of the three acts. It deals with the effort to resolve the conflict established in act one through the actions of the characters with whom we've come to identify.

In *Die Hard*, this is Bruce Willis's effort to rescue the hostages and the twists and turns that happen along the way. In *Speed* it is the effort to get the passengers off the bus, while making sure it doesn't go slower than fifty miles per hour. In *Taken* it is everything that Neeson does to rescue his daughter from her kidnappers.

In other words, act two is actually the "story" part of the movie. It is the bridge from the introduction of the characters and the conflict...to the characters resolving the conflict. It's where all the "good stuff" happens in the middle that makes you care about what happens in the end.

ACT THREE

Act three is the resolution of the conflict. It is Bruce Willis rescuing the hostages, killing the bad guy, and regaining the affection of his wife. In *Speed*, it is the fight on top of the subway train that wipes out the villain, and the rescue of Sandra Bullock. In *Taken*, it is Liam Neeson rescuing his daughter from the human traffickers who have sold her into captivity.

This same "three act" formula works for all kinds of movies. For example, in a romantic movie, the three-act concept works the same way.

In the Tom Hanks film, *Sleepless in Seattle*, act one is where Hanks, a single father, ends up talking on a radio station because his young son makes the call. Meg Ryan hears him and has a strange connection with his voice and sincerity. (It introduces the characters and sets up the conflict: these two must get together.)

Act two is all the things that happen to keep this couple -- who should obviously be a couple – apart from one another. (It is the effort by the characters to resolve the conflict.)

Act three is the scene on the observation deck of the Empire State Building where our star-crossed lovers finally get it together, and they go on to "live happily ever after." (It is the heroic resolution -- pass the Kleenex.)

The Memorable Conclusion

In the movies (or TV or novels) there is almost always a well-defined, heroic resolution. The guy gets the girl; the warrior kills the evil force; the cowboy in the white hat wins the duel with the one in black. In real life, however, we seldom get to spike the ball after scoring the winning touchdown ... or ride off gallantly into the sunset with the wind at our back.

This helps explain why we are often our own worst storytellers. We enjoy and repeat the myths of other corporations and professionals -- and fail to see *our own*.

It's our fault. In this high-tech, high-stress time, we don't allow ourselves to revel in the achievements we have attained. We don't tell the story, even to ourselves. We simply hurry on to the next event, and we miss the satisfying ending that was waiting to be noticed. We fail to celebrate, and we also fail to communicate to the world the conclusion of our triumph.

As we try to understand our stories, part of our problem is that we hope that our "final chapter" is not written for a long, long time. We don't want to think we've reached the end of the story. However, if our hero is eternally trapped in his or her trials, eventually we lose interest. We want to see movement.

So, to create a compelling conclusion, try to think of it this way: the end of your story may be a beginning of something new and exciting in your business. In other words, the end of one story prepares you for another – the sequel, if you will.

Satisfying endings are emotional. We want to cheer as you spike the ball or ride into the sunset.

The problem in business is that many companies and professionals have failed to see how this format creates a story that is more compelling and emotionally connecting for their customers and employees.

Your business is show business – so begin to craft a three-act story that will have your customers cheering! We love to read stories that contain emotion -- but when writing our own story, we tend to neglect it. Don't settle for a dry recitation of facts. Find the drama -- and the emotion -- at the heart of your story.

Solidify the Vision

Vladimir Lenin was an astute observer of cultures and economies. While we may – or may not -- disagree with his favorite form of government, he did make a very powerful statement about our free enterprise system.

Lenin said, "Capitalism thrives on the shrewd manipulation of
_____"

* *Wait a minute!* Let's examine how your thinking has progressed...
* What do you think is the key element to Lenin's statement?
   o Capitalism thrives on the shrewd manipulation of *workers*?
   o *Capital*?
   o How about *the economy*?

* **What Lenin said is that, "Capitalism thrives on the shrewd manipulation of _imagery_!"**

Perhaps this is a way of saying that -- even at the time Lenin was writing -- he realized that all business would become "show" business.

Lenin could not have foreseen the dominance of the entertainment industry. Nor would he have envisioned the electronic media playing such a role in the people's perceptions of their government and its leaders. However, it is obvious from the statement, Lenin understood the power of stories and the importance that imagery plays in developing a story that emotionally connects with the intended audience.

Here is a question for you. After you have answered it, ask around your office and see if your colleagues have the same answer as you. Who were the most popular 20th century Presidents of the United States?

Most people will answer that the most popular two American Presidents of the last several decades are John F. Kennedy and Ronald Reagan. (Public opinion polls would also include Bill Clinton somewhere near the top of the list as well – and let's speculate on that selection in just a moment.)

We have discussed the importance of show business in customer (in this case, _voter_) decision-making. So, is it any real surprise that the two most popular Presidents of recent times were the ones who were best able to manipulate imagery?

On several occasions, I had the opportunity to meet and work with a former event planner for President Reagan. The members of the Reagan White House were masterful when it came to creating visual imagery for the evening news.

This former White House staff member told me that the Reagan White House believed every public appearance by the President gave them a chance to show and share Mr. Reagan's vision.

Each speech by the President was planned with the great care and meticulous nature of a movie set. Everything had to appear just perfect, I was told.

The reason is because the imagery made a much more powerful impression than the words Mr. Reagan used to communicate. People would remember what they saw on television more than they would remember the words that had been spoken, or the ideas that had been discussed.

Again, let me emphasize I do not necessarily think that this is the way that things *should* be. However, it is the way things *are*. Effective and persuasive business professionals operate in reality -- even if they sometimes find that reality challenging.

President Kennedy was ahead of his time in understanding the power of imagery. From his dramatic speech at the Berlin Wall, to allowing the press to photograph him while boating and playing touch football with his children, Kennedy projected a youthful and virile image.

This was quite a contrast for a nation accustomed to the lack of images -- or the bland imagery -- presented by Kennedy's predecessor, Dwight Eisenhower.

Lyndon Johnson did not understand the importance of imagery. Richard Nixon understood it, but could not master it. Gerald Ford and Jimmy Carter were unable to communicate a vision. George Bush (the father) even joked on occasion about his inability to communicate "that vision thing."

The American voters elected only one of these men more than once. Interestingly, the one elected twice was forced to resign from office. (You have to wonder -- would Richard Nixon's fate would have been exactly the same if he possessed the style and ability to make emotional connections like Bill Clinton?)

John Kennedy brought Hollywood to the White House (and, in more ways than mere imagery, evidently).

Ronald Reagan's great success and popularity could be attributed, in large part, to his use of "show business" principles in the public sector. Given the dramatic cultural changes we have been discussing in this book, do you think it mere *coincidence* that the most popular President of recent times was a movie actor?

Is it sheer happenstance that the biggest Presidential electoral upset of recent years involved a media-savvy, former reality television show host, who – throughout his career as a real-estate developer – used his media skills to build his brand and his own name recognition?

The Bill Clinton presidency will be discussed and debated for many years to come. Perhaps no other President has such a polarizing and diverse standing among Americans – at least until the current Chief Executive.

While this is *not* a political book, Bill Clinton serves as a useful example in any study of the power of stories -- and the need to understand the significance of images.

While many joked about Bill Clinton telling people that he "felt their pain," the fact remains that he did so convincingly. So compellingly, in fact, that even though he is (as of this writing) only the second American President to ever be impeached, he now commands fees of $150,000 and more to speak and relate stories to corporate audiences.

(Obviously, he is speaking to corporate groups – who else could afford a $150,000 speaker?)

Clinton was so masterful at telling stories and using imagery to project his vision, that many were willing to overlook his shortcomings and transgressions. You and I may disagree about his policies and principles. I just do not think there is any doubt, however, that in Bill Clinton we observed the Michael Jordan of retail politics.

One must wonder what Hillary Clinton could have achieved at the polls had she possessed the same ability to connect with audiences and tell stories as powerfully as her husband – or other renown and revered global leaders ranging from Indira Gandhi of India, to Golda Meir of Israel, to Margaret Thatcher of the United Kingdom.

And the point is...

What does this have to do with *your* business?

If you want to get your message across internally -- and you want to have the effectiveness (and yes, popularity) required of a leader to get things done -- then you must focus in detail on the images that you are presenting.

• • •

<u>Show Biz Quiz</u>

* What are the images that you and your organization send out? Are you conscious of them?
* Do you have a vision for the future of your organization?
* Are you using imagery to project and illuminate the vision – to tell your STORY?

• • •

Another critical reason that explains why "ALL business is show business" is because it is no longer "tell" business!

Today's customers and employees do not want you to *tell* them anything! To expand on our previous example -- Kennedy, Reagan and Clinton all used stories to make important points memorable – and controversial points palatable.

Even in Biblical stories cited in the text revered by those of the Christian faith, Jesus appeared to understand that compelling stories have more impact, and are therefore more memorable.

We remember the images of the Good Samaritan and the Prodigal Son. It seems that in today's vernacular, "Verily, verily, I say unto you," could be translated into, "You know, that reminds me of a story…"

Customers and employees want you to have a vision for the future -- and how your products, services and employment will impact theirs.

The only effective way that you can communicate this is to engage them – *tell them a story!*

This can either be through a narrative that is so vibrant that you are drawing "word pictures" for your audience -- helping them visualize the message you are conveying, regardless of the method or media used to transmit the communication. Or, with presentation technology, you can use actual images -- just as a movie director or television newscast would -- to relate your vision of the story to your audiences.

What we are discussing here could be looked upon as two separate aspects:

1. How we communicate our stories more effectively through the way we manipulate imagery; and,
2. The development and communication of our corporate vision.

Yet, I do not believe that the two are required to be separate at all – in fact, we communicate more compellingly when these two points are connected.

* **While it is imperative in today's world to communicate the vision you and your organization has for the future, you must remember that an inappropriately, ineffectively and inadequately communicated vision is the same as having no vision at all.**

By the way, if you still are not convinced about the importance of imagery in communicating your show business, consider the words that we use to describe great leaders. They are said to have "*insight*," and "*vision*."

When we comprehend what they communicate, we state that we can "*see* what they are saying" -- and when we understand them, we "get the *picture*."

The military of the United States learned the hard way about the need to manipulate imagery.

The unfettered access of the press bringing the Vietnam War home to American living rooms every night was one of the main reasons that public support for that conflict waned so dramatically.

On the other hand, the military completely controlled the images of the first Gulf War under the command of General Norman Schwarzkopf -- and maintained strong enthusiasm and public support throughout that conflict.

And, as you probably know, the military has even been accused in more recent conflicts of crossing the line -- from "controlling" images, to "manipulating" them – in order to sell the American public on their version of the story.

Yet, this continues to make our point. The United States military leaders would not be so committed to this effort unless they firmly believed it would have a dramatic impact upon the results created by the influence on the American people of a compelling story.

The Director as Manager/Leader

The power in stories and images -- and the emotions they create for employees -- has significant implications upon how managers run a business and leaders guide their teams.

First, it means that today's best metaphor to use for managerial excellence is not some athletic coach exhorting the team to "give 110%."

(Which is obviously impossible, anyway. If you give 100% -- that's *all there is*.)

I was speaking for a meeting not too long ago where the sales manager must have thought he was the reincarnation of Vince Lombardi. Every old cliché in the book was thrown at the poor sales staff.

"There is no 'I' in team!" he shouted to his troops.

"No, but you can find *two* of them in 'idiot,'" I thought.

"We're going to cross the goal line and spike the ball on the competition!" he exclaimed. Meanwhile, one female on the back row turned to a friend and pretended to insert her finger down her throat. I seriously doubt that "regurgitation" was the action that the sales manager was hoping to inspire.

Come on, how many more "sports as life" metaphors are we going to have to sit through?

Don't get me wrong -- I am a huge sports fan, to the point of being a fanatic for the Indianapolis Colts.

However, in today's more diverse workforce, "football" to many employees means what we call "soccer" in the United States.

And, how many times after a meeting where "sports" serves as the theme does an organization turn to something different that would appeal equally as well to non-sports enthusiasts for next year's event?

Please don't misunderstand me – I'm not suggesting for a moment that a love of sports is restricted to the male of the human species. I am just strongly suggesting that when we seek a metaphor that provides the imagery and emotional connection we're looking for to communicate a powerful message, we need to appeal across a broad spectrum.

* **We can use show business.**

A better example of a real manager and leader is the director of a film.

It is someone like Steven Spielberg – a leader who can talk in highly precise terms with the members of the crew involved in the technical aspect of filmmaking, yet utilize emotion and motivation to get the best performances out of the cast of the film.

It also implies that we deal with different people differently. You wouldn't direct Arnold Schwarzenegger in the same way that you would direct Anthony Hopkins.

(I just had to smile thinking about Anthony Hopkins saying, "I'll be baaak." Then, I realized the only thing funnier would be Arnold saying the line from *Silence of the Lambs* about a "nice Chianti and fava beans.")

Another area of dramatic impact could be discovered in the internal training of employees and colleagues. Training and education, in many cases, is going to have to change.

Training is usually conducted trying to change and enhance the *behavior* of people in the organization. In other words, we train people to get them to conduct themselves in a manner in which they were previously unfamiliar or underperforming.

* **"Show business training" understands that a better metaphor is the employee perceiving himself or herself as an actor or actress performing a role.**

This approach makes directing (managing) much less threatening to the employee and much more effective for the organization. You encourage your colleagues in their performances *without criticizing them as individuals.*

If I, as a director, ask an actor to play the role in our organizational story a little differently, it does not mean that I have any less respect for them as a professional or a person. I'm just trying to get something a little different for my movie, play – or business!

One of the challenges I often see is that many companies ask their employees to provide customers with a level of service that the employee has never experienced as a customer! Training a person to provide a level of service of which they are unaccustomed is a challenge for any organization.

For example, a bellman at the Four Seasons probably has not been required to take a business trip like the one you are on when you check in. Nor has he or she likely been able to afford the kind of pampering you are there to enjoy. Yet, you expect the bellman to give you "Four Seasons" type of service.

The woman behind the counter at the dry cleaners I used to use just didn't understand why it was such a big deal that they didn't get my suit ready when they promised.

"Don't worry," she tried to assure me, "you can pick it up tomorrow morning." The fact that I was getting on a red-eye flight at midnight and wouldn't be in town tomorrow morning just didn't register with her. She was so used to thinking that everyone works 9-to-5 (after all, she does!) that my situation was outside her frame of reference.

What you are showing me prevents me from hearing you...

People believe -- and respond – to what they *see* long before they respond to what they *read* and *hear*. That is another reason why stories are so important – words, data, facts are conveyers of information. Because stories engage us emotionally as well as intellectually, they create an impact that is visual – we "see" it in our "mind's eye."

The mind tends to remember what it visualizes much more effectively than facts or figures that it memorizes. You'll <u>never</u> walk up to someone and say, "I remember your name – but, *your face escapes me!*"

We recall the face, the image – we just don't recall the words, the associated name, that accompanies it.

That's why you remember the earlier story about the father with the daughter in the accident that was saved by the Ajax Widget – but probably forgot that the first example explained that it came with a five-year guarantee.

Have you ever been checking out of a department store like Kmart? (I use this specific example because it was the first place I noticed the visual phenomenon described here.)

The 18-year-old kid turns to you at the end of the transaction, makes a half-hearted attempt to smile a fake smile and in a droll, disinterested manner says, "Thank you for shopping Kmart."

Do you believe the cashier is thrilled in <u>any</u> way about your patronage? *Of course not!* You believe they have been *trained* to say this. Just like the dolphin jumping through the hoop at Sea World, the Kmart cashier thanks you "for shopping Kmart." *Zap! Zap! Zap! Zap!*

Here is the reason the words make no positive impact: While the words were the correct ones to say to a customer, the visual (in other words, the uninspired look on his or her face) is what you almost always choose to believe.

• • •

<u>Show Biz Quiz</u>

* What is said to YOUR customers right after they have made a purchase?
  o Is it part of your UCE?
* Do they believe what is said because there is congruency between what is said and the story/images you project?

* When was the last time that you – or a friend who doesn't work with you – played "Mystery Shopper" and did business with your organization?
* When was the last time you called your own number to see how long you would be placed on hold – if the operator did not know it was you?
* How about your employees? What is said – and shown – when they perform at an exceptional level?
* When was the last time you watched the old movie, "Planes, Trains and Automobiles" – and used it as a way to teach and re-learn the value of customer and personal relationships?
    o Can you do it again tomorrow?

• • •

Making the vision visual

So, how do you solidify and share your vision through a compelling story?

First, you had better *have* a vision for what the future will bring. You had better be able to "see" how your business will become show business -- and strategize methods for communicating this to your customers and employees.

* **In other words, distinctive leaders make their vision visual.**

Second, you must understand that the vision is best related through the power of story.

A statement I make during my presentations that always seems to receive profuse agreement from the audience is this:

* **We get so busy *doing* what we do; we never have time to *think* about what we do.**
    o *Have you fallen into that trap?*

A story can provide that "recess to reassess" we all need. In other words, your narrative can become the bridge that takes away us from the worries and concerns of the moment, and into a better frame of mind so we may be more productive in our planning, our ideas, and our strategies for execution.

Take these steps:

1. Put a few flip charts around you in your office.
2. Start visualizing what your vision is for the future.
   a. Maybe you will use words to describe this vision, or maybe draw small pictures.
3. The time you invest in being a "visioneer" will pay back incredible dividends to your organization -- and you.
4. Next, work on developing a story the creates a compelling description that illuminates, explains, and inspires the listener about the vision you have created.

Storyboarding

An effective technique that show business uses to develop and refine the vision into a structure that can be communicated as a captivating parable is called "storyboarding."

While most of us are familiar with scripts or screenplays, many of us are not familiar with the storyboarding process. Before any movie is filmed, artists literally draw a picture of each scene of the film. They develop a book that is an illustrated version of the movie that is prepared prior to filming.

The storyboarding process allows the director, producers, stars and craft people working on the film to "see" the film in their heads and understand more clearly the director's vision of the work.

This principle can -- and should -- be applied to business as well. Too often we give instructions and directions about what we want -- without storyboarding so our customers and employees can "see" what we are saying!

Here's an example: The cashier mentioned in the earlier illustration has probably been told to "smile and thank the customer." Perhaps they have been provided the specific words they are supposed to say to express the corporation's appreciation for patronage.

What has probably not happened is for the organization to "storyboard" the process for the cashier. In other words, share the vision of why this is done -- and stress the importance of "delivering the line" in the appropriate manner to the cashier. If that cashier first sees an example of the performance delivered as desired, and then is provided specific direction on how to mold their performance to the same standard…guess what happens? *You get a better performance!*

Using storyboarding to solidify the vision gives your employee/"actor" a chance to see the performance that you are encouraging.

How can you develop a business storyboard?

The two main methods that I would suggest are:

1. *Illustrations.* Find an illustrator to literally draw the vision that you have for your organization or department, or the actions that you would like to see exhibited by your employees.
    a. This might be easier to do than you imagine. Most major metropolitan areas have a plethora of talented artists waiting for the opportunity to do corporate work. You might consider having them draw a series of cartoon panels showing what you want your organization to achieve.
    b. It is no coincidence that the bulletin boards most frequently read are the ones that have cartoons posted upon them. Use e-mail or social media as a method of distribution of illustrations that clearly show your vision for your organization.
    c. Your storyboard about the positive outcomes that you want to receive and the kind of behavior that you want to encourage can become a series of illustrations…or, maybe even a comic strip!

2. *Video.* With all the amazing changes in technology in the last few years, it is *easy* for you to create and produce your own small video productions. Depending on your time and budget, you may want to use an outside video production house. There are many excellent shops to be found across the country.

    a. Or, perhaps you may want to develop a team activity where you make your own production that, in essence, creates a movie -- based on the storyboard that you have developed -- to explain your vision or encourage the desired performance.

    b. Staff members would have fun creating their own "home/corporate movie." At the same time, they will be growing, learning and communicating in a manner that reinforces exactly what you want.

Even if you start a world-famous business from the proceeds of your first Social Security check, your business will depend upon both the quality of your product...and the essence of your story.

In 1959, Harland Sanders took the $105 dollars from that check, and lived in his car as he drove from town to town, restaurant to restaurant, telling his story of the "secret recipe of eleven herbs and spices" that made his chicken so delicious. By 1964, there were more than 600 locations selling Kentucky Fried Chicken.

Remember, because your business is show business, your success in the future could depend on your shrewd manipulation of imagery – and by how effectively that you tell *your* compelling story.

• • •

<u>Show Biz Quiz</u>

* When was the last time you did an image audit?
    o What are the images that your colleagues see every day when they come to work?
    o Do they portray the "best" of your organization?

* What images inspire you the most?
  o For some, it will be a basketball player dunking the ball. For others, it may be a seagull flying over the ocean surf.
  o Visualize them – then write them down.
* How can you incorporate these questions and/or your visions in a way that your colleagues find inspiring?
* What action steps can you take to become a "visioneer"?
  o And, what are you waiting on?

• • •

Chapter 8

● ● ●

Pacing and Focus: The Keys to Ongoing Involvement

*N*ot long ago, I loaded a disc into my DVD player, and watched in horror. Here was what I thought must be one of the worst public speakers in the world making a presentation.

Following his introduction, this guy sprinted up to the stage and started his presentation at a ridiculously high energy level. He then attempted to continue to maintain that level of energy throughout the entire hour-long presentation!

He started out talking too loud…and got louder. He started out talking too fast…and got faster.

Evidently, he believed that if his speech was rapid enough, he could get more of his points in the presentation. It was the audience's damn fault if they couldn't remember them because they blazed by so quickly! It seemed he must have thought that if he were loud, the points he had to communicate would seem more important – as if mere volume determines significance.

This speaker had done his research on his topic area -- and he had a great passion and belief in his subject.

But, what he evidently knew nothing about was the importance of *pacing* in a performance. His passion and belief -- as well as his ideas and concepts -- were lost to the audience amid the sound and the fury.

Because "ALL Business is Show Business," you must learn what that speaker should have known: you can discover the key to audience attention and involvement in the pacing and focus of your communication.

So – I stopped the DVD and hit the "Eject" button.

I shook my head and thought, "I cannot believe the guy on the video was...*me*." It was a program of mine from many years ago.

My problem was at the time of that presentation, I did not yet understand one of the most important concepts in show business. Neither was I aware that it also had significance to the way that any business – or individual professional -- should communicate. It's the issue we'll explore in this chapter.

Ebb and Flow...

Few singers begin their concerts with their biggest hit songs. They understand that there is an ebb and flow in the emotional impact of a performance, and you must keep your audience wanting more.

You must establish the pacing for *your* performance. My mistake in the early days of my speaking career was to assume that I had to begin my program with a high degree of energy -- *and maintain it* -- to preserve the attention of the audience.

This is important to the "show business" organization. In today's highly stressed, rapidly changing times, one of the challenges transpiring is that people are quickly becoming "burned out." Customers are getting burned out on the places they do business.

It seems to me that the life span of many organizations has been shortened merely because customers grow weary of doing business with them. They want something fresh -- they want a change.

A friend of mine who owns a nightclub in the Midwestern region of the United States did a major revision of his club. He changed the name and the décor, as well as the music that was performed there. His customers had grown tired of the former concept after a short two-year period.

When I asked him about the different clientele he was attracting with his new concept, he replied, "Oh no, it's the *same people* that came before. They just wanted a different experience."

Pacing is a method that helps you prevent employee and customer burn out. It is the way that you ensure your products and services have a longer shelf life, and that you are able to achieve some degree of balance, as well.

The Three Acts of YOUR Business

Earlier, we discussed the "three act" approach to storytelling. Now, let's use those three acts to take a look at pacing and focus, as it regards a customer's interaction with your business.

If your business is retail, for example:

1. Act one: They enter your location and a conflict is established. They ascertain the character of your business from the images that you are projecting. They have entered your location because of a conflict -- there is something that they want or need to purchase, or a problem they need to solve.
2. Act two for the customer is their effort to resolve that conflict. They will seek out what they want or need. They become involved with other characters in the presentation (your employees) as they seek a resolution.
3. Act three is the conclusion of their experience. Both you and they hope that this "movie" has a happy ending -- one that ends in a successful completion of the transaction. (Not to mention a "sequel" of repeat business!)

Now, add the element of "pacing"

Show businesses must analyze the customers' experience in each of the three acts. They must understand the role that pacing plays during the resolution of the conflict that is created when the customer seeks to do business.

The appropriate pacing varies from one business to another.

If you are a fast food restaurant, for example, the entire course of the pacing will be much quicker than if you are a gourmet establishment.

Again, however, it is insightful to think about how this applies to movies. If a movie is paced too quickly, the audience tends to lose its focus. They can't keep up with everything that is happening on the screen and they become disinterested.

Some recent films that have tried to dazzle and amaze their audiences with a rapid-fire succession of special effects have bombed at the box office. The reason?

First, these films have not given us enough of a chance to meet the characters and identify with them.

One of the oldest clichés in sales is that "people do business with people they like to do business with." While times are changing, this is an adage that is still quite true. The rationale is the same reason that we identify so strongly with the films that we have been discussing.

In *Taken*, we identify with Liam Neeson -- we like him, we identify with him as a parent, and we want to see what happens to him. Movies that pace too quickly at the beginning do not give you the opportunity to make a connection with the characters.

Also, when the pace is too quick in act one, the audience becomes a little "shell shocked." They haven't had time to settle in and prepare themselves for what is about to happen.

This can happen in business, as well. Organizations that pace too quickly at the beginning do not allow their customers to make a connection with them.

Have you ever walked into a fast food restaurant where no one else is in line, and as you are merely approaching the counter, the clerk loudly asks you for your order? You just aren't ready to decide yet, but you pressure yourself to come up with your order because the clerk seems impatient. You *want* to go, "Wait a minute. Let me catch my breath." The pacing has been too quick and sometimes you sit down with your food and think, "why did I order this?"

If the pace is too slow, the audience becomes disinterested. If the movie drags on, we don't care too much about what happens to the characters. We are bored.

* **It seems to me that one of the worst things that any movie -- or any business -- can be is *boring*.**

* Have you ever had to stand in line so long at the grocery store that you practically stopped caring if you got the groceries or not?
* Have you ever left your cart – with the merchandise you were going to purchase – behind in a department store because the line was so long you didn't want to take the time to check out?

As I was thinking about and preparing this chapter, I was looking for a place to have lunch. I drove into one fast food establishment, walked into the restaurant and saw the line was very long. I thought the pacing would be exceedingly slow, so I walked back out of the restaurant, got into my car and drove to a second establishment. There, too, the line was very long. I returned to my car and drove to a third restaurant. By the time I got into the third restaurant, I got in line and waited. It dawned on me that had I merely waited in line at the first restaurant, I would already be eating.

However, the impulse to resist a pace that is too slow is almost overwhelming.

Customers want it right!

Doesn't there seem to be some kind of inherent conflict here? I am telling you that, as a customer, I don't want you to wait on me too quickly – on the other hand, don't make me wait, either!

It's almost like the story of the Three Bears – we want it "just right!"

Organizations need to evaluate the pace at which they deal with their customers and employees.

Remember the principle:

* *If the pace is too rapid – if there is too much going on -- customers and employees "burn out" and lose focus.*
* *If the pace is too slow, customers and employees become disinterested, start thinking about other things -- and lose their focus, as well.*

One of the things that I always try to do in my professional speaking presentations is to take the audience on a "roller coaster ride." Because of what I learned from that experience watching myself on the DVD, I mean there should not be a simple, linear progression from one point to another. My goal as a speaker is to create a series of peaks and valleys.

Sometimes I will talk quietly and slowly to pull the audience in. Other times I will speak louder and faster with much more animation to my gestures. This variation in pacing maintains the audience's attention. It pulls them up and lets them down – it keeps them interested intellectually and emotionally.

Examine your business through your customer's and employee's eyes. Is there variation in pacing -- or is it the same old thing every time? Are you using the pacing of your customer contacts to make certain that the customers focus upon what is important?

* Is your customer focusing upon what you want them to?
* How about your employees?

Learning focus the hard way

I learned a very valuable lesson about focus. I had a presentation to give at an early morning meeting in Springfield, Illinois. Springfield is not a long drive from Indianapolis, where I lived at the time, so I had dinner at home with my wife. Then, I packed one suit, one pair of shoes, one tie and one shirt for the presentation. I took off, driving for Springfield. I arrived at my hotel about 9:30pm.

As I entered in my room and began to unpack, it hit me like a ton of bricks! I had brought the *wrong shirt!*

Unintentionally, I had packed a shirt with French cuffs. In my head, I could visualize my cufflinks on top of my dresser back in Indianapolis.

I try to bring a lot of energy to the platform and use a lot of gestures when I speak. Not having cufflinks would be horrendous! I would make a broad, sweeping gesture and my cuff would flap out and slap someone in the head. This would be *terrible*!

I knew I had to find cufflinks. I ran down to the gift shop in the hotel where I was staying, only to find that it had already closed for the night. I dashed across the street to the Hilton to find their gift shop was closed, as well. I raced back to my hotel and ran up to the bellman.

"I have a terrible problem," I exclaimed. "I have got to find some cufflinks!"

"Are you kidding me? Where do you suppose you can get cufflinks in Springfield, Illinois at 9:40pm on a Tuesday night?" The bellman's answer about late night shopping in his small home city was *not* helping me solve my problem.

"Well," he said, "the only two places I can think of that are open this late are Walmart and Target department stores. They are both open until 10pm -- but they are on the other end of town. It will take you 20 minutes to drive there. You *might* make it."

I jumped in my car and felt like a Formula One race car driver as I made my way through the streets of Springfield. Running red lights, squealing my tires, I pulled up in front of Walmart just 15 minutes later. Dashing into Walmart, I asked the "greeter" at the front of the store, "do you have cufflinks?"

"You might try over there in jewelry," he slowly answered. When I dashed up to the jewelry counter and made my request, the expression on the clerk's face told me everything I needed to know about Walmart's inventory. They did not have cufflinks.

Running back out to my car, I jumped in and hurried directly to Target department store. Sprinting into Target, I heard the announcement that it was 10pm, and customers should immediately bring their purchases to the front.

I caught the eye of a sympathetic cashier and exclaimed, "Cufflinks!"

She pointed me in a direction and shouted, "Men's Department!"

I raced back to the Men's Department, and skidded up to the counter. Out of breath, adrenaline pumping, I practically screamed at the poor clerk, "Do you have cufflinks?"

"No!" she said as she recoiled from me.

Dejected, I turned away and muttered under my breath, "Oh, no! What am I going to do?"

"Sir," the clerk called. "Is it really important?"

I turned around and explained how I had driven over from Indianapolis, brought the wrong shirt and was going to have to give my speech tomorrow without cufflinks.

She smiled sweetly, and asked, "Well, *why don't you just buy another shirt?*"

* *It had never dawned on me to get another **shirt**!*

Has your organization ever done anything like that? Have *you* ever made a similar error? Have you ever focused so much on the symptom – the cufflink – that you weren't focusing on the real problem?

So many times, I see organizations that focus on tasks that need to be done -- instead of centering their thoughts and actions upon their employees and customers.

Paul Cole, global director of the customer relationship management team for Cap Gemini Ernst & Young, was quoted in *Fast Company* magazine as saying that, "Since the Industrial Age, we have been building a business model that was designed to help people create, produce, and deliver a product to the market. But that business model wasn't designed to deliver an enhanced customer experience. Until we get marketing, sales, and customer service converging in a way that adds value, we're going to keep disappointing the ultimate customer."

Unfortunately, this, too, is a sign of the "cufflink" mentality.

* In movies, if your audiences are focusing on the special effects instead of the story, you are in trouble.
* In your business, if employees are focusing on the cufflink instead of the shirt, you are in a similar jam.

The hotel desk clerk that gets reports completed to please the manager rather than taking immediate care of the guests exhibits the "cufflink mentality."

The organization that will not allow its salespeople to take calls from customers while they are holding sales meetings exhibits a similar lack of proper focus. It's another sign of the "cufflink mentality."

* **Balance must be reached in all excellent forms of entertainment – and in <u>your</u> efforts -- in terms of focus and pacing.**

The challenge for your "show business" is to keep the focus where it needs to be. And, you must establish a pacing that will keep things moving – yet, maintain your audience's interest.

• • •

Show Biz Quiz:
Here are a few questions to conclude this chapter.

1. Have you thought about pacing in your organization?
   a. How can you change the pacing to enhance interest yet avoid burnout within your organization?

2. What are the three acts that customers go through when they encounter your organization?
   a. Try to outline the three steps:
      i. act one: the initial contact with your business
      ii. act two: their search for resolution to their conflicts and desires
      iii. act three: the successful ending.
   b. As you examine these steps that customers take, you will begin to see different alternatives for serving them and creating the kind of experience that will make them want a sequel.
3. Where is the real focus in your organization?
   a. Is it on the "cufflink" or the "shirt"?
      i. What can you do to redirect the focus to make certain that it is in the right place?

● ● ●

Chapter 9

As the Curtain Rises

The points I have been making throughout this book were driven home to me by a stockbroker in Manhattan.

We were chatting about the challenges she had been facing in her business because of the volatility in the stock market, combined with the economic impact of the tragedies of September 11, 2001.

She refused to let the events that were happening dictate to her the level of professional success she was going to attain.

"When I went through my training to become a broker," she told me, "just about everything we learned was about the *products* we would be selling to our clients. Mutual funds, stocks, bonds, annuities, and so forth. I wasn't having much success getting my career off the ground, so I went to a sales training program. There I learned many techniques to close a sale -- features and benefits, rapport building, forty ways to secure agreement -- stuff like that."

"Frankly," she continued, "it didn't improve my business all that much. Then I realized that *anyone* could learn those tricks. And *everyone* has product. What no one else could duplicate was *me!*"

"Every time I talked to a client or prospect," she said, "I was on stage for them. My passion, my commitment, the experiences I could create for clients and prospects -- I realized I had a monopoly in the marketplace on *me!*"

When the stockbroker in Manhattan said those words, a powerful simplicity in her phrases struck me. From computers to cars, from furniture stores to flower shops, from General Electric to a general store, everybody has product.

> *   **Yet, as she so eloquently implied, it is what you do <u>beyond</u> product that makes all the difference in business.**

Please do not misunderstand what I am trying to say; having a superior product is incredibly important and powerful.

Yet, no customer is loyal to a product.

Customers become loyal to the experience that is created by the mixture of the product with the service, feelings, benefits, and advantages they encounter as a result of their use of the product.

Managers often make mistakes because, like the Manhattan stockbroker, they do not connect what they have been taught and trained to do with what the changing marketplace desires.

Several basic errors contribute to our inability to create compelling experiences for our customers and our employees.

Here are three:

1. Working harder at the old plan
2. Placing economic connections before emotional connections
3. Believing that "price is king"

Error #1: Working harder at the old plan

The "work ethic" is praiseworthy. However, never before have we seen people working so hard and so long with so many tools to accomplish so little.

When production goals aren't achieved, the natural assumption that most managers make is that we must "bear down and work harder." The whip is cracked and often there is hell to pay.

I've seen many sales managers tell their salespeople that they aren't "making enough calls." Of course, that's the old plan; more calls mean more sales, right? As we now know, the answer is, "Not necessarily."

* **If your current strategy -- which may have worked beautifully just a short time ago -- isn't creating the results needed in today's market...why work harder at the old plan?**

A company that has been a client of mine has two divisions that each sell a product through the same distributor network. In other words, both Division A's product and Division B's product are retailed through the independent offices of another company; we'll call it the XYZ company.

Division A assigned a large number of salespeople to small territories who would frequently visit XYZ. They took a very aggressive selling approach and focus totally on the product. Division A constantly demanded more and more calls from their salespeople. The philosophy was "burn and churn"; if some salespeople couldn't stand the pace, they would leave and be replaced. Product was the king, not the people.

Division B took the show-business approach, building emotional relationships. They employed a much smaller team of professionals, but Division B made a strong commitment to their people and set up compensation plans that encouraged them to develop partnerships to help develop the business of the XYZ Company. They started a speaker's bureau and provided the services of consultants and experts to assist the professionals of XYZ in building their profitability.

In turn, emotional connections were created between XYZ and Division B that fostered loyal relationships. Because of the relationships and emotional links, XYZ felt very comfortable selling the product of Division B.

Division B is selling millions of their products; Division A is still trying to gain access to the real decision makers at XYZ.

Perhaps most important, the divisions will soon be merged, with the manager of B having total responsibility. The president of the parent company wants the show-business approach implemented throughout the organization.

The manager of Division A recently said he just "wished the market was better and his people had worked harder." He still doesn't get it.

Don't just "think outside the box." Plan and *do* outside the box!

Error #2: Placing economic connections before emotional connections

Obviously, if your organization doesn't succeed economically, it has no viability. However, many managers fail to understand that emotional connections precede economic ones. If you get the emotional connections in place properly, the economic associations will follow.

Even those companies that advertise that they are the "low price leaders" within their respective industries still must create positive feelings and trust about doing business with them before customers will sample their low prices.

Businesses are constantly evaluating how they are doing from an economic standpoint -- and they clearly should. Many companies, however, spend no time judging how they are fulfilling customer and employee needs from an emotional standpoint. That must change.

The problem in business seems akin to that in medicine. Future doctors spend an enormous time in medical school learning the technical skills of their profession. And don't get me wrong -- that's a great thing! I want the doctors who treat my family and me to have a superior amount of technical skill. However, they receive little training in the aspect that will be one of the most important of their medical careers: managing their personal, emotional relationships with patients.

Whether we acquire our business acumen through university courses, in-house corporate training, practical experience, or a combination of all three, precious little time is spent on a fundamental aspect that will allow us to create distinction for our organizations and ourselves.

> * **It is critical that we develop the skill of managing our personal, emotional relationships with clients and colleagues.**

Remember the old cliché: Before they care how much you know; they have to know how much you care.

Error #3: Believing that "price is king"

Price matters. There's no doubt about it. Naturally, I want to pay a competitive price for anything and everything I purchase. I want to make a good deal and I don't want to think I have paid more for something than someone else who has chosen the exact same thing. That's a normal and natural part of consumer behavior.

Still, price isn't all that matters, no matter what some think.

Take drinking water as an example. Water is free at water fountains in every public building and park. Just go to your tap and turn it on. Did that stop Evian or Perrier? Did they say, "Well, who would pay for water?" Absolutely not! They created a unique perception about their product.

By the same token, did Starbucks say, "Wait…you can get coffee just about anywhere? Why would people go out of their way to get it from us? We'd better be the cheapest or else they won't make the effort!" Just the opposite! In fact, you could argue that in the case of Starbucks, high price is a differentiating factor; it's part of the aura of their success.

If other organizations can make coffee and drinking water into products for which customers are willing to pay a premium, what excuse do you have that you can't do the same with your products and services?

> * **Many of the challenges we face when it comes to pricing stem from our inability to creatively develop strategies that differentiate our products and services in a manner that provides a compelling emotional experience to the customer.**

As we discussed many times in this book, customers crave distinction.

If you don't create uniqueness for the customer, they'll provide their own. And, here is the easiest way they know how: by asking for a cheaper price.

However, when you realize you are "on stage" -- that ALL business is show business -- you can create such a compelling emotional connection that you can make anything (even water and coffee) a highly unique experience.

Here are seven additional points that will help you better accomplish your goals:

#1) Determine your business

When beginning a seminar, I will often ask professionals to answer this simple question: "What business are you in?"

Naturally, most will answer with a pretty standard, and specific, definition. "I'm in the car business," for example.

My response is to say that the "car business" is your industry, *not* your business. When you understand what business you are involved in, you hopefully avoid the errors we've just discussed...

Here are three businesses in which all of us are involved:

1. *The emotion business*
2. *The perception business*
3. *Show business*

The emotion business

You have specialists who manage the financial and economic aspects of your organization, yet you probably haven't given too much thought to the management of the emotional aspects of your company. How your customers and employees *feel* about you, your department, your organization, and your business could be more important than the facts about what you do.

When the airlines were cutting employees by the thousands after the terrorist attack of September 11, 2001, local television stations in Los

Angeles broadcast a story about some American Airlines employees who had worked for the airline for two decades; according to the story as it was reported, they were fired by E-mail from the corporate headquarters. The employees -- who were also told to continue to work at local ticketing offices in the L.A. area for a few additional days -- were shown on camera weeping as they were helping customers.

Even if you give American the benefit of the doubt that the cost-cutting measure was economically necessary, wasn't there a better emotional way to handle the situation? What kind of feelings did this action create among other employees?

The action was so troubling that it made me less likely to fly American. If, after more than twenty years of service, an employee cannot be treated with dignity, what does that say for the treatment a customer will receive? How can the airlines expect their employees to be of service to customers and encourage loyalty, when they know they can't count on it from their employer? Apparently, no one thought about that.

Companies are going to have to learn that they can make decisions that are economically correct – however, if they implement them in a manner that is emotionally bankrupt, they will pay a steep financial price. You are in the emotion business.

* **The way you obtain loyalty from customers and employees is, in part, through the strategic creation of positive emotional experiences.**

The perception business

We have heard experts on communication say that "perception is reality." However, we have often failed to understand that principle when it comes to business.

Perception about the future value of a company drives its share price on the stock market. And perception motivates the kind of loyalty we want to acquire from customers and employees.

For many years, I flew a large number of miles on United Airlines. After an incredibly bad service experience, I stopped giving United my business. I know it tracks my frequent flyer miles, because I get periodic online statements.

Couldn't United easily have had a "red flag" on accounts that showed a dramatic drop in business?

Yet, after years of loyalty, I never received a note from the airline asking, "Where did you go? What can we do to get your business back?" As a result, my perception was that it obviously didn't care too much about my business -- or else it would have wondered where it went!

However, if it had inquired, my perception would have been totally different; I would have felt like somebody noticed. That would have made a giant impression.

> *   **Are you tracking customer loyalty? Are you creating the right perceptions about how much you care?**

In the first edition of this book, I mentioned that I did a lot of work with a company that had just hired a new CEO. He had plans for turning the company around – and they were strategies that made great economic sense.

However, he was perceived by most in the organization to be someone who does not care about the people who work for him. Therefore, he received neither the productivity nor the commitment from the very people who were essential in the execution of his plans.

In the original text, I wrote, "I do not believe his company is going to make it. I also believe the reason it will not isn't because of his economic strategy, but rather the perception of him by his colleagues is so bad that few want to be on his team."

Sadly, that prediction turned out to be right. (And, it's one that I really wish I would have gotten wrong!) The company failed – not because of inferior strategy, but because of negative perceptions about the leader trying to implement it.

People won't get on board with you if they perceive you can't get them where they want to go. However, you will be amazed by what they will do if they perceive you can deliver what they want. Revolutionary products and services are created by leaders who, like the late Steve Jobs for example, can inspire the perception that people are a part of something "insanely great."

Show business

I'll say it here one more time: whatever your product or service, in today's world you must realize that your business isn't just about what you do -- it is about the performance you give when you are "on stage" before customers and employees, and how that serves to create experiences they want to repeat.

During the economic downturn experienced at the onset of the 21st century, the food service business reported a dramatic rise in customers for those restaurants that served "comfort food" -- meat loaf, steak, and potatoes, the old standards. Why? Because restaurants aren't just about food; they are about experiences.

State Farm Insurance, to use another example, could simply say "Give us money now, and we'll give your spouse a check when you die." Instead, of course, they tell us that they're "like a good neighbor." The success of this High Concept goes well beyond a mere slogan. It means that my State Farm agent realizes she is "on stage" every single time we talk about my insurance needs; she needs to convince me she is a "good neighbor." She needs to deliver a performance that will satisfy not only my financial requirements and plans -- but also my need for an emotional experience that will make me want to come back and buy more insurance...and send my friends to her for their policies.

Any actor realizes that no matter how she feels, or what has happened in her personal life that day, or what kind of mood her cast mates are in, or what the weather is, or how large the audience is for that day's show -- despite all these factors, each and every performance must be executed with perfection and passion. It is her responsibility to use her training and talent to create an amazing experience for the audience.

I want the managers where I buy my stocks and bonds, rent cars, service my computers, and eat and sleep overnight -- and on and on -- to understand the very same thing.

I want them to emphasize that fact -- and inspire similar perfect, passionate performances -- with their employees.

#2) Get a performing partner

Show business is full of examples of superstars getting their start by working closely with others.

From Dean Martin and Jerry Lewis, who worked together as a comedy team before their individual successes, to Eddie Murphy, Kristen Wiig, Adam Sandler, and other former members of the cast of Saturday Night Live, show business knows that creativity and productivity are often enhanced through collaboration.

If you're a young professional, find a mentor. If you happen to be a seasoned professional, locate some young rebel. Share the ideas in this book that have appealed to you and work together to create concepts specific to your organization. Stimulate unique thinking and motivate each other to action.

Hold your partner responsible for getting things done -- and have him or her do the same with you.

#3) Contemplation creates a superior presentation

I've presented more than two thousand speeches in front of audiences as large as 25,000 people -- and yet I am always nervous before I go onstage.

My mentor in the business, the late Grady Nutt, always used to tell me, "It isn't nervousness -- it's 'performance anxiety.' You want to do a good job, so you are anxious. Take some time and get your thoughts together."

Taking some time and getting our thoughts together is a great idea before any performance, no matter the stage. We have all seen performers who have great command when they perform. They fill up the arena in concert; they jump off the TV or movie screen with their charisma. You need to have this kind of control of the situation whenever and wherever *you* perform.

To achieve this power, every entertainer and speaker that I know will take just a moment before the performance to "get centered" and become "audience-focused." They take that time to get into the mindset necessary for presenting the best performance possible.

Develop a checklist of what's important. Take a quick look prior to every call, staff meeting, or review. This doesn't take a lot of time; it merely takes the discipline to stop for a moment and center your thoughts -- and yourself.

When you are passionate about your topic, you can easily get carried away. Some professionals have become so excited about their favorite concepts that they run the risk of turning their colleagues off to their ideas. They need to take a few moments and contemplate before they present their thoughts.

My speech coach was the late Ron Arden of San Diego. He always said, "You should never speak from the heart."

That's a shocking statement when we want to be passionate and compelling with our "show biz" communication. But Arden went on to counsel, "You should write and prepare what you have to say from the heart. You should *speak* from your skill."

Develop your communication to employees and clients from your heart and emotions. Then, present the communication after contemplation. Focus on your skills.

#4) Maintain performance shape

I had the thrill of seeing Elvis Presley in concert during his first tour of the early 1970s. Even though I was young, I still remember it like it was yesterday.

It was an amazing show -- Elvis prowled the stage like a panther. He showed off his karate moves and danced and sang without ever losing a beat. He was absolutely mesmerizing.

I will never forget talking with my mother on the phone after she had attended an Elvis concert several years later.

By this time, Elvis was overweight, couldn't move without becoming winded, and at one point even lay down on the stage, flat on his back, to sing a song.

My mom was crushed. He was no longer the Elvis of her dreams; to her, he was now just an out-of-shape, middle-aged man.

Have you ever seen an action movie that was unintentionally funny because the star was out of shape and obviously couldn't do the stunts he was pretending to do on the screen? Part of creating emotional connections is projecting a sense of congruency. You'll have a harder time convincing clients and colleagues that you are focused if you eat, drink, and smoke too much. What people see speaks more loudly than what you say.

This isn't a "fitness book." And I'm not suggesting that you must look like Tom Cruise or Halle Berry to be successful in your "show business." I certainly would be accused – rightly – of not practicing what I'm preaching; I'm not in that kind of shape, either.

However, you and I must remember that we are in the perception business. Fair or not, we presume that fit companies are managed by fit people.

As my friend Michael LeBoeuf says, "If you don't invest the time to be healthy, you will have to make the time to be sick."

#5) Focus upon success; learn from failure

During the interviews that I conducted with many celebrities during my days as a movie reviewer, it always impressed me how the superstars kept a constant focus on what they vibrantly desired to achieve in their profession.

John Travolta told me he read every single script that anyone gave him. Arnold Schwarzenegger started several little businesses before he became famous so that he would have an income stream that meant he didn't have to take insignificant acting jobs just to keep food on the table.

We've all heard and read the many other stories of present-day stars who waited tables and worked as carpenters so they could continue to pursue their dreams while dealing with the rejection of failed auditions.

The lesson you can learn from them is to practice a dual focus on the success you want, while learning from the failures you encounter.

* Keep your High Concept in front of you.
* Repeatedly examine your story.
* Relentlessly refine your UCE strategies.
* Constantly ask yourself this question:
    o "What specific action can I take today that will help me and my organization profitably create experiences that our customers and employees want to repeat?"

And meanwhile, understand that things won't always work out the way you want. That's why we must commit ourselves to making failure our laboratory for future success.

Every change we make -- especially when it comes to changing our philosophy of business -- involves risk. As one prominent advertising campaign said, "The greatest risk is not taking one."

When we change, we risk. When we risk, we sometimes fail.

However, when we learn from our failures, we pave the road to success.

In his book *Failing Forward,* John Maxwell states, "In life, the question is not if you will have problems, but how you are going to deal with them. Stop failing backward and start failing forward!"

In part, the way you "fail forward" is to take responsibility and learn from each mistake.

#6) Don't let the critics grind you down

When the entertainment scene was my responsibility, I always referred to myself as a "movie reviewer" rather than a "movie critic." The difference may seem insignificant, but, as I've mentioned often, it had a subtle power for me.

The term "reviewer" implied to me that I was going to go to a movie, then tell my television audience what my impressions were about the film. I was free to get enthusiastic about what I liked -- as well as tell my viewers what I found disappointing.

I went to each movie -- a minimum of one per week for over ten years -- with the hope and expectation that I was going to see something worthwhile.

A "critic," on the other hand, seemed to me to be someone who went to the film with the *intention to criticize*. He or she would search for what was wrong so they could tell their readers or viewers about the movie's weaknesses.

Many of the so-called "critics" I knew played the game as if it were a blood sport. They loved taking famed directors and actors to task. For a few, I suspect that disparaging some of the successful performers they critiqued made them feel a little more successful and worthwhile themselves.

We see the same phenomenon in business every day, and you will notice it even more as you shape your organization toward the "Show Business" approach. If you let the critics have their way, you will never accomplish the fundamental changes in your organization that today's culture requires.

Sometimes, we erroneously presume that the critics know what they are talking about. That is not always the case.

"Can't sing. Can't act. Can dance a little." That was one critic's impression when he saw Fred Astaire for the first time.

In your business, you need to know the difference between the reviewers -- who will tell you the good and the bad – versus the critics, who only want to criticize.

#7) Bridge the "do" gap

Relatively few businesses actually *execute* strategies that will enhance their organizations.

As I said earlier, we get so busy doing what we do -- and so caught up in the office politics, or suffer from the "cufflink" mentality that I mentioned in a previous chapter -- that we do not accomplish nearly as much as we could and should.

Many years ago, I heard a speaker talk about the fact that we do not have an information gap in business. He said we have a "do gap." We do not lack for information; we are deficient in execution. As business philosopher Jim Rohn once said, "We major in minor things."

The director shouts an important word..."ACTION!"

To make a difference, the concepts in this book must be *applied*.

Why do we continue to talk about the same business leaders over and over -- Bill Gates, Warren Buffett, and the late Steve Jobs, for example? Because these individuals rocked the boat. They and their companies provided examples for changing times.

Too often, however, we learn the lesson intellectually and fail to implement it strategically. We fall victim to the "we've never done it that way before" syndrome.

Motivational speaker Anthony Robbins says that "Motion creates emotion." This implies that if you want to create emotional connections with customers and employees, you have to *move*!

The challenge is this: do something! When I pick up the Bible of my particular tradition and faith, I find no chapter called "Wishes" or "Hopes" or "Dreams" or "Wants." There is one, however, entitled "Acts." Even 2000 years ago -- just as in the times of today -- a challenge facing individuals was to *act* on the knowledge they held in their minds and the beliefs they held in their hearts.

When they did, they changed the world.

You, too, can be an "act-or" -- one who takes action

Thoreau wrote, "Most men lead lives of quiet desperation." I believe that many men and women -- executives and entrepreneurs, supervisors and staffs -- lead careers of quiet complacency. These times call for something different -- something dramatic! If you don't rock the boat just a little, it will eventually sink.

As the curtain rises on your production – on your time in the spotlight with your "show business" -- your challenges are to:

* Create a High Concept statement that is short, attention grabbing, powerful, and unique.
  o Develop such an interesting statement that listeners can't help but ask you to tell them more.
* Using the High Concept as your foundation, craft a powerful story that creates a compelling case for customers and employees to become connected to your organization.
  o Use your history -- combined with your vision of the future -- as a promise to your customers and employees.
* Design the Ultimate Customer Experience (UCE).
* Deliver upon the promise of your story and engineer the systems necessary to create this experience for every customer, every time.

Because of the power of its message, I conclude all my speeches with the following poem. It applies here – and to you – as well:

• • •

Tomorrow

He would be all that a mortal could be
Tomorrow.
No one would be kinder or fairer than she
Tomorrow.
Each day he would stack the letters he would write
Tomorrow.

She'd think of the clients she'd fill with delight
Tomorrow.
But the fact is they died and faded from view…
And all that was left when their living was through…
Was the mountain of things they intended to do
Tomorrow.

-EDGAR GUEST (ADAPTED)

● ● ●

Remember the "ALL Business is Show Business" philosophy as a five-step approach to making your business – and you – more compelling in the marketplace:

1. Begin to perceive YOUR business as "show business" – and that your goal is to create distinction through compelling emotional connections with customers and colleagues
2. Develop a High Concept for your company, department, specific projects – and yourself – to enhance the precision of your focus and become exceedingly clear about your uniqueness in the marketplace, who you are, and what you can deliver.
3. Craft a persuasive story (or stories) to deepen and enrich emotional connectivity with a more powerful and memorable approach.
4. Pay special attention to the pacing of the customer's interaction with you – and how that can focus their attention in a manner that will obtain mutually successful outcomes.
5. Prepare yourself – and educate your team – in the techniques of performers creating emotionally engaging experiences, not just as employees executing the functions of their jobs.

TODAY is the day…it's **SHOWTIME!**

Let's Keep in Touch!

I truly believe that the "show business" metaphor strikes at the heart of what all businesses need to create distinction during these changing times.

That is why I issue you an invitation -- and a challenge. The invitation is to visit our web site at http://CreateDistinction.com. On our website through my blog, I will provide updates of what managers, entrepreneurs, executives, and all employees are sharing with me as I travel the world presenting programs on the subject. I hope you'll enjoy the ongoing content and information!

And, your final challenge: here's to attaining rave reviews, developing constant sequels, creating marketplace distinction, and earning standing ovations from your customers and employees!

Join Us in Distinction Nation!

Become a part of an exciting community dedicated to creating distinction – personally and professionally – and integrating the "ALL Business is Show Business" approach in everything we do.

Distinction Nation provides the clear, straightforward resources required for you to stand out and move up...regardless of your field of endeavor or goals for the future.

With monthly videos and members-only podcasts – as well as monthly webinars so you can get your specific questions answered directly by Scott McKain – as well as an annual, "live" Distinction Summit – there are fantastic benefits to being a part of Distinction Nation!

For more information – and to sign up for membership – go to:

http://DistinctionNation.com

Contact Scott McKain...

If you would like more information on Scott McKain's unique speeches and seminars, consulting services, impactful training programs delivered both in person and through a highly interactive online format -- and other projects of assistance to organizations seeking to create distinction and discover more about how "ALL business is show business" – contact:

Distinctive Presentations, LLC
5371 San Florentine Avenue
Las Vegas, NV 89141

+1-800-838-6980

Shelley@ScottMcKain.com

Or, contact your favorite speakers bureau!

Visit our websites:

http://ScottMcKain.com

http://DistinctionInstitute.com

http://CreateDistinction.com (blog)

http://ProjectDistinct.com (podcast)

Acknowledgements

Neither this book – nor any of the speeches and other wonderful opportunities I have -- would have happened without the extraordinary belief and dedication of Shelley Erwin. Her official title is Chief Operating Officer of our company – and I'm grateful beyond description for all that she does in so many ways.

(Last, but not least, she's also the "world's greatest sister.")

I also appreciate the others in our small organization – especially the work of Benjamin Amick, who edits video and audio, contributes to our website, helps keep the wheels on the business, and does an all-around great job.

Thanks, too, to Perry Cremeans for his diligent efforts for so many years.

Every two weeks, four of my best friends and I post our comments on a random subject that we all find interesting. What makes it most fun is that these commentaries from The Five Friends (TheFiveFriends.com) have become very popular! I love each of these guys – and I'm privileged to be their friend. Thanks Larry Winget, Mark Sanborn, Joe Calloway, and Randy Pennington.

This project initially became reality thanks to Thomas Nelson Publishers and my literary agent, Mel Berger of William Morris Endeavor, who remains a tremendous inspiration to me. He is one of the true legends in the publishing business.

Bruce Johnston has been a great colleague, friend and advisor. I'm grateful to him, as well as his wonderful wife, Dawna.

No one could have better professional colleagues than I possess with my fellow members of Speakers Roundtable. Their generosity is amazing – and their friendship beyond description. It is such an honor to be a part of this group.

Thanks, as well, to the speakers bureaus and clients across the country that keep my calendar full.

Heartfelt appreciation to the best buddies a guy could have – my pals in the greatest band in the history of country music, Diamond Rio.

Thanks to Brian Prout, Dana Williams, Gene Johnson, Jimmy Olander, Dan Truman and Marty Roe. You guys rock! (But, not too much – you're a *country* band!)

The Oak Ridge Boys are not only country music's greatest group and Hall of Fame inductees – they have been supporters, mentors, and friends since my teens. They are still delivering what their audience REALLY wants at the shows they perform throughout the world each year. Joe Bonsall, Duane Allen, William Lee Golden, and Richard Sterban – and, of course, road manager Darrick Kinslow – I want you to know how much I appreciate your friendship and encouragement.

My gratitude, as well, to the many authors and speakers who have given me ideas and assisted in the development of both the concept and the manuscript behind this book.

My appreciation, too, to my two stepsons, Corbin and Faron – and Corbin's wife, Amber…and their new edition to our family, young Calvin! You will have an unlimited future if you'll deliver what your customers *really* want…regardless of the field in which you work in the future.

Finally, my heartfelt gratitude to my wonderful wife, Tammy, for being such a loving and gentle presence in my life. It's great being teammates through life together with you.

Most importantly – thanks to YOU for taking your time to read this book. I sincerely hope it has been of value.

About Scott McKain

Scott McKain is an internationally known authority who helps organizations create distinction in every phase of business and teaches the "Ultimate Customer Experience."

Scott McKain's keynote presentations benefit from three decades of experience, combined with his innate talent for articulating successful ideas. McKain has spoken before and consulted for the world's most influential corporations.

Scott McKain creates captivating presentations and bestselling books which clearly reveal how to create more compelling connections between you and your customers and how to stand out and move up, regardless of the economic climate in your industry.

Scott is the founder of the Distinction Institute, a consulting and training company that explores the role of ultimate customer experiences in creating enhanced client retention and revenue, and is the author of three Amazon.com #1 business bestsellers; all teaching how to expand profits, increase sales, and engage customers.

He has presented his business strategies on platforms in all fifty states and seventeen countries...from Singapore to Sweden; from Mexico to Morocco...from the White House with the President in attendance; to conferences in Dubai and Abu Dhabi.

He was recently named to join Zig Ziglar, Seth Godin, Dale Carnegie and just twenty more in the "Sales and Marketing Hall of Fame." He has been honored with induction into the "Professional Speakers Hall of Fame."

And, he is a member of "Speakers Roundtable" — an elite, invitation-only group of twenty business speakers considered by many to be among the best in the world.

Professional Facts About Scott McKain

* The Miami Herald and about thirty other leading newspapers named Scott's book, *Create Distinction*, as one of the 'TEN BEST BUSINESS BOOKS' of the year.
* His keynote presentations benefit from three decades of experience, combined with his innate talent for articulating successful ideas.
* He has spoken before and consulted for the world's most influential corporations.
* Scott is the founder of a consulting and training company – Distinction Institute -- that explores the role of ultimate customer experiences in enhancing client loyalty.
* He is the author of three Amazon.com #1 business bestsellers; all teaching how to expand profits, increase sales, and engage customers.
* He has presented his business strategies on platforms in all fifty states and seventeen countries...from Singapore to Sweden; from Mexico to Morocco...from the White House with the President in attendance; to conferences in Dubai and Abu Dhabi.
* Board of Officers and Directors of a half-million-member educational organization
* Board of Directors of National Safety Council
* Board of Directors of a multi-million-dollar charitable foundation
* Founder & Owner of a training company with a multi-million-dollar interactive online platform
    o Clients include the world's most progressive corporations including BMW, Bank of America, ING (India), Juniper Networks, and many more
* He has been honored with induction into the "Professional Speakers Hall of Fame."
* He has also been inducted into the "Sales and Marketing Hall of Fame," joining Zig Ziglar, Seth Godin, Dale Carnegie, Napoleon Hill, Earl Nightingale, and just 18 others.

Other Interesting Facts About Scott McKain

* His hometown of Crothersville, Indiana named the section of US 31 Highway that passes through the center of the community as "Scott McKain Way," in honor of their favorite son's achievements in publishing, speaking, broadcasting, business, and philanthropy.
* Arnold Schwarzenegger personally booked Scott for a program on the White House lawn, with the President of the United States in the audience for his presentation.
* By the age of 21, he had met with the Chairman of General Motors in GM's Boardroom in Detroit and with the President in the Oval Office – inspiring a fascination with business and leadership that continues to this day.
* Scott had weekly commentaries syndicated to television stations around the world for a decade, seen weekly by over two million people, and has interviewed most of the leading celebrities.
* He has sat in on drums on multiple occasions with a platinum selling, Grammy winning band, and counts several country music stars as among his best friends.
* Scott is a veteran of media – with multiple appearances on FOX News Channel and NBC's "Today" show, has been quoted on many occasions in the *New York Times, USA Today,* and *Wall St. Journal,* and has appeared multiple times as a commentator on FOX News to discuss business, politics, and American Culture.
* He was a news anchor for a CBS-TV affiliate in one of the nation's 25 largest markets.
* Scott played the villain in a film from the auteur that *Time* magazine called the "world's greatest living director." The movie was named by the late Pulitzer Prize winning critic, Roger Ebert as one of the "fifty greatest films" in the history of cinema.
* *GenJuice* magazine named Scott (along with Biz Stone of Twitter and Mark Zuckerberg of Facebook) as one of the "top 20 people that young professionals should follow on social media."

* *Social Media Marketing Magazine* named Scott as one of the 25 most influential marketing authorities on Twitter.
* Scott has a YouTube video of a speech story that has been watched by well over 100K viewers – that caused McGraw-Hill to invite him to write a book about the story.
* Scott has been named as a "Hoosier Hero" in his home state because of his commitment to youth and philanthropy.

www.ingramcontent.com/pod-product-compliance
Lightning Source LLC
Chambersburg PA
CBHW051648170526
45167CB00001B/385